A STONE MADE SMOOTH

WONG MING-DAO

OMF BOOKS
404 S. Church St.
Robesonia, PA 19551

A STONE MADE SMOOTH

WONG MING~DAO

MAYFLOWER CHRISTIAN BOOKS

The Publishing Branch of

MAYFLOWER CHRISTIAN BOOKSHOPS CHARITABLE TRUST
114 Spring Road, Sholing, Southampton, Hants.

ISBN 0 907821 00 6

Cover design and line drawings by Ruth Goodridge
Typeset by Print Co-ordination, Macclesfield
Printed in Great Britain by Stanley L Hunt Printers Ltd.
Midland Road, Rushden, Northamptonshire, NN10 9UA

Contents

Preface

Publishers Preface

Introduction

CHAPTER [

1 A brand plucked out of the fire 1

2 Separated from my Mothers womb 26

3 Through fire and through water into a
   wealthy place 51

4 A fortified city, an iron pillar
   and a bronze wall 85

5 Overseer of the flock 113

6 Give them something to eat 142

7 I will make a helper suitable for him 156

8 Learning from each other 189

9 Memories of my Mother 203

10 We must obey God rather than men 210

11 Smooth stones 240

Preface

For many years I have lamented the pitiful dearth of information available in English concerning leaders in the Chinese church. Christian writers have tended to focus on Western pioneer missionaries, often failing completely to show the commanding influence of Chinese pastors, evangelists and theologians. Biographies of Chinese church leaders in English are scarce indeed, and translations of their important representative writings even scarcer. Watchman Nee is the lone exception.

It is thus gratifying that Arthur Reynolds has laboured hard to redress this imbalance. His choice of subject is singularly fitting. Born in Peking in the year of the Boxer Uprising, Wong Ming-Dao is Chinese through and through. In fact, one may describe him as a true exemplar of the principles of "three self" —

self governing, self supporting, and self proclaiming. No Christian Chinese leader in the twentieth century has more clearly articulated the power of the Gospel of Jesus Christ, or more poignantly experienced what the Apostle Paul described as "the fellowship of sharing in his sufferings". Released after twenty-three years of imprisonment, he told how the words of the prophet Micah had sustained him.

> But as for me, I keep watch for the Lord,
>   I wait in hope for God my Saviour;
>   My God will hear me.
> Do not gloat over me, my enemy!
>   Though I have fallen, I will rise.
> Though I sit in darkness,
>   The Lord will be my light.
> Because I have sinned against him,
>   I will bear the Lord's wrath,
>   Until he pleads my case
>   and establishes my right.
> He will bring me out into the light!
>   I will see his justice.

James H. Taylor III

Publishers' Preface

We are so thankful to be able to publish this remarkable story of the first fifty years of the life of Wong Ming-Dao, told in his own words. It was about twenty years ago when I first received some of his "Spiritual Food Quarterlies", which made a deep impression upon me. I had never read anything quite like them; their pastoral understanding and penetration was to me unique. His stress on Christian conduct meets a real need that is so lacking. I tried to find out where I could obtain more copies of his writings, but to no avail. About eight years ago, a friend told me of Arthur Reynolds' interest in the writings of Mr Wong, and I made up my mind, some time, to contact him. This I eventually did, and Mr Reynolds, in his Introduction, has explained what happened. We are extremely grateful to Arthur

Reynolds for his untiring labours. It has not simply been a question of translating from the Chinese, but gathering material together which was not originally intended as an autobiography. This has meant careful editing. It must be stressed, however, that nothing of any importance in Mr Wong's writings has been omitted. Editing has only been done where there has been obscurity or repetition. Incidentally, most readers will have been used to Mr Wong being described as "Mr Wang". Arthur Reynolds, however, has laboured meticulously to be accurate at every point, and this has included the spelling and pronunciation of Mr Wong's name. He is presently engaged on translating Mr Wong's "Spiritual Food Quarterlies", which we hope to publish soon by instalments, a sample of which is included at the end of this book, entitled, "Smooth Stones". The title of this book itself, *"A Stone Made Smooth"*, has been chosen by the publishers themselves as Mr Wong himself, it will be noticed, refers several times in his life story to being like a stone made smooth. Indeed, it has been his own experience. Also, the article entitled. "Smooth Stones", describes the way in which David killed Goliath with a stone that had been made smooth, and it is a fitting picture of the way in which Mr Wong has been both prepared and used by God in a special way. Mr Wong would most certainly not describe himself in this way since it would appear presumptuous, but it is quite appropriate for others to use this title, which is so suitable, for his story.

We have been in contact with Mr Wong and he is pleased to know that we are making his writings known in English. It needs to be said, however, that he has not taken any initiative in arranging for the publication, nor has he checked the translation. The responsibility for the publication, therefore, rests entirely with the publishers. It should be added that Mr Liu Yih-ling, of United Gospel Literature, Berkeley, California, has kindly reviewed and checked the translation. We are thankful to him for his help here. We also acknowledge the valued help of Mr David Adeney of the Overseas Missionary Fellowship. The O.M.F. themselves are very kindly co-operating in the distribution of this volume. This is most fitting because of the interest shown by the O.M.F. in Mr Wong, and their bond of fellowship. We are especially grateful to James Hudson Taylor III, General Director of the O.M.F., grandson of Hudson Taylor, (the founder of the O.M.F.) for his readiness to write such a helpful Preface to the book. His commendation is most appropriate. Readers will find so much in the book that is of value that it may seem out of place for me to draw attention to any one aspect of the book. However, Mr Wong undoubtedly has an emphasis, and this is clearly on the matter of Christian conduct, and the need for a godly example. Surely, this is both Biblical and represents an area that is so lacking in these days. So much is being done in the name of Christ that seems to lack depth. There appears to be such a need for the type of things that Mr Wong has been so able to say. We trust, also, that this autobiography will whet people's appetites for his own writings when they shortly become available.

David Fountain
on behalf of the publishers

Introduction

Over twenty-three years without a Bible! Over twenty-three years without Christian fellowship! Over twenty-three years without normal Christian activities! And no letters except from his wife!

This is what lay behind the Lord's servant, Wong Ming-Dao, when in January 1980 he was released from prolonged confinement in Peking — a confinement imposed by the former authorities. He was almost eighty at the time of his release and though weak in body he was still strong in spirit. We know little of his experiences over these years, but Brother Wong himself is satisfied since all is known to God.

Where can we learn the secret of his steadfastness in the face of strong and unremitting pressures? We can learn a good deal from what he himself has shared with us in earlier autobiographical articles published in his magazine, 'The Spiritual Food Quarterly'. Some of these writings, necessarily condensed, are presented here in translation. I have sought to remove passages and to arrange some material more chronologically.

A chapter which makes thrilling reading has been added from one of Mr Wong's other books. It describes his experiences during the occupation of Peking by the Japanese army. I myself once lived in an occupied town in north China and I can appreciate what Mr Wong writes of that period, particularly the prevalent fear of the military police. I may add that I have also worked with the Lord's people in Japan and I am aware that many of their leaders suffered considerably, during the war, also through the policies of their government. As with Brother Wong so with them — they faced persecution as a direct result of choosing to obey God rather than men.

When I began translating Mr Wong's writings with a view to publication in the mid-1960s I felt strongly that the had a message for us in the West. That is why I have kept up this translation work, as time permitted, ever since. In the early part of 1979 I received a letter from Pastor David Fountain, the minister of Spring Road Evangelical Church, Southampton, when he expressed a desire to publish some of these translations. This publication is the result.

It was nearly a year after this proposition that Wong Ming-Dao was released. His wife, Jing-Wun, had also been sent to prison, and kept there for twenty years, but she had been released earlier. She has always made a powerful contribution to her husband's ministry. Her spiritual insight, her remarkable courage, and her Christ-like patience are clearly brought out in this record.

Twice only did I have direct contact with Brother Wong Ming-Dao (though I was a reader of his magazine for years). I once heard him preach in a large and crowded hall in Nanking, and so impressed was I that passages in his message remain with me to this day. On another occasion he was the visiting speaker at a convention of Christian students, and he graciously let me talk with him as he sipped a glass of milk between two sessions. This time it was the man as much as the message that impressed me.

Although Mr Wong normally ministered at the Christians' Tabernacle in Peking, he was always in great demand as a speaker at special meetings, both devotional and evangelistic, all over China. It was not uncommon for him to spend six months in the year away from his church in Peking. He was absent, as it happened, when I attended a service there, and the preacher — if I remember correctly — was a Netherlands diplomat, a Mr Kok, who was a member of his congregation.

Mr Wong Ming-Dao, to me, is not simply a remarkable leader. He is one of the outstanding preachers of the century, and in saying that I am thinking of three vital elements in preaching — man, message, and method (or presentation). This is not to suggest that he has no shortcomings. In fact he frankly speaks of them in this testimony. Nevertheless he is a warrior who, with singleness of purpose, takes little account of possible wounds; he is demonstrably prepared and willing to lay down his life for his Master.

Arthur Reynolds, 1981

1.
A brand plucked out of the fire...

I began my life in extreme poverty. Few people indeed have known circumstances so pitiful. I have never discovered where my forebears came from; the name of my paternal grandfather and what he did for a living are alike unknown to me. I have no idea whether others in my clan are still alive. My father died early and my mother had made no enquiry about these things. I only know that my father's name was Wong Dzu-Hou and that he came to Peking as a young man. He worked at the Tong-Pen Hospital which was run by a missionary society. My father and two other gentlemen spent part of their time studying and part of their time working, and eventually became doctors in the hospital. My father was over thirty when he married my mother. Following the birth of my eldest sister, another daughter and then a son were born, but both in turn became ill and died. Another boy died at birth. The fifth child born to my mother was myself. My mother's family name was Li and her personal name was Wun-I. When 10 years old she had been a pupil at a Girls' School in Peking run by the London Mission (London Missionary Society). That was about 1880.

In the year 1900 came the bitter suffering of the Boxer Uprising. The Empress Dowager accepted the reports of foolish officials and encouraged the so-called Boxers by offering them rewards to kill all foreigners and Christians. This led to catastrophe and the allied armies entered Peking. The streets of Peking were thrown into chaos and all the foreigners in the city took refuge in the Legation Quarter. Chinese Christians followed them. Amongst them were my father and mother with their small daughter, my elder sister. The Boxers surrounding the Legation were joined by troops of the Ching Dynasty and together they fired into the Legation area with guns and rifles. While this was going on my father climbed a ladder to the top of the wall where he could see outside. When he came down he told my mother that there was a strong force of Boxers and Government soldiers outside, and that sooner or later they would be able to force their way into the Legation. This report aroused the fear that those inside might suffer a cruel and painful death. Would it not be better to take their own lives first? So it was that, not long afterwards, someone brought the news to my mother that my father had strangled himself. He was buried without delay. My mother and father had only been married for six or seven years when she was widowed in this way. I had not yet been born at that time and my mother was left with a little girl several years old.

The fighting became daily more serious. Refugees were crossing the river from the east to the west. And it was in this place of refuge, on the 29th day of the 6th month of the lunar calendar (July 25th on the solar calendar) that my mother gave birth to me. It was not possible at such a time to get the help of a midwife, and the place of midwife was taken by my grandmother. When she saw that I was a healthy boy she was very pleased, and she gave me the name 'Iron'. When I was small the name did not please me, but later on I was called by God to serve Him and I read what He said to the prophet Jeremiah (see chapter 5): 'I have made thee this day a defenced city, and an iron pillar and brasen walls against the whole land . . They shall fight against thee but they shall not prevail against thee (Jeremiah 1:18,19). After reading that, I recognized the greatness of the name given to me in infancy. The name given to me by my grandmother was according to the will of God.

At the time I was born my father had already been dead for one month and three days. Not only did I never see my father but I did not even see his photograph, for at that time it was only very rarely that people had photographs taken. And those that had been taken were lost in the upheavals of that period. To have lost my father in that way was very distressing, but thanks be to God the misery of that time eventually gave way to the joy of today.

After the turbulent events of the Boxer Rising died down the refugees were able to leave the Legation and return to their homes. Some had no home to go to. My father, while alive, had worked at the Tong Ren Hospital and had lived inside that compound, but now that he was dead it was, of course, impossible for my mother to continue living there. It was necessary for her to find accommodation elsewhere and she rented a small house in Gan-yu Hutong (Hutong means 'lane').

Although my mother when young had been a student at a Girls' School run by the London Mission she was not equipped on her own to handle business affairs. With a girl of 5 or 6 and a small baby boy she was even less able to go to work. Fortunately the church received indemnity funds after the Boxer Rebellion and she was given several hundred ounces of silver with which to support herself and her family. After some time the house we rented was put on the market and my mother had sufficient money left to buy it.

Life at home

After some time, as my mother's money got less, she was able to rent out some of the rooms and use this income to maintain our livelihood. But with two small children it became more and more difficult for my mother to support us. Every day we ate maize flour or some other coarse grain. Another problem was that my mother greatly disliked cooking. Sometimes we had only one meal a day. When the pangs of hunger became most acute we went on the street and bought a few baked cakes. When my mother became older she often declared that she preferred to go hungry than to occupy herself cooking. Indeed the death of my second elder sister was ascribed to her not eating meals at the proper time and of then becoming ill with hunger. This was not to say that mother was lazy. From morning till night she was unwilling to take even a short rest. She liked washing clothes and doing needlework; she liked

sweeping the rooms and the courtyards. And she was happy reading the newspaper. In fact the only thing she did dislike was cooking food. So when I was young the food I ate was never good and we never ate our meals on time. I naturally suffered physically and was frequently ill. We were fortunate that my grandmother lived with us for a number of years and she often took charge of our meals. Otherwise we might have become more seriously ill through hunger, as my mother herself acknowledged.

The small rent my mother received was naturally not enough to meet the living expenses of three people. After a few years my mother acted on advice to convert an outbuilding into a room that could also be rented out. Thus our income was slightly increased. Later on my mother still had enough money in her possession to put up other rooms.

Close neighbours

My grandmother and my aunt were living with us and there were eight other families, making a total of about 30 people living together in the courtyard. Although this arrangement brought an increase in rent it nevertheless caused many problems and difficulties. Our neighbours were often unreasonable and rowdy. We had no adult men in our family and we had no particular standing, so the tenants took advantage of us. They would fail to pay their rent; they would act insolently; they would go around cursing; they would form gambling groups; they would engage in shady activities. My mother, as landlady, was in a dilemma. Should she intervene or not? Suppose she kept aloof. If anything untoward occurred the landlady would have to take responsibility. But what if she intervened? In all probability they would refuse to take any notice. Moreover my mother had a tempestuous nature and any altercation with the neighbours never ended with a few words but resulted in violent loss of temper. In view of this she tried to restrain herself and say nothing. When the situation became impossible to endure she became so worked up that she made herself ill.

She debated with herself whether to give up renting out the rooms. But that would mean giving up our only source of income. On the other hand, when we rented out the rooms we had to accept the inconvenience of having close neighbours. Unhappy widow and orphans! This was our existence for years. In those days I was too small to appreciate my mother's love or to sympathize with her, but I realised she found it hard to make a living. I used to take a basket or a sieve and go to the places outside well-to-do houses where they dumped the rubbish. I collected enough rubbish to take home and to use it to make a fire and in this way we could reduce slightly our expenditure on fuel. I carried on doing this for many years. Even when I started school I would collect rubbish in the morning before I went off to school with my bag of books. Only when I was 12 and became a boarder at the school did I give up this chore. In the winter we used a stove made from an old kerosene tin for both cooking and heating. My clothes were thin and my hands and feet were frozen. My hands were so cracked and painful it was almost impossible to use them for writing.

An enquiring mind

Even from my earliest days I was always keen to learn. I constantly took a book to my mother and asked how a particular character was pronounced or what its meaning was. My mother did not spend much time in teaching me but I was always asking her questions.

Not only did I like reading but I also liked to turn things over in my mind. I pondered many common problems and the one that most depressed me was, 'What really is the meaning of human life?' 'Where do people go in the future? Is there anything beyond death?' These are the questions I addressed to various people. Invariably they replied, 'All must die.' But as to what happened after death their replies were very varied. Some said, 'Dead, dead, dead, and that's the end.' Some said, 'When people die it's like extinguishing a lamp.' Some said, 'Air changes into wind and flesh changes into dust.' Still others said, 'After you die your spirit will go to King Yen (the King of Hell) to be judged. The good go to heaven but the bad are bound in iron chains by small demons to receive all kinds of bitter punishment in hell. Still others said, 'After death a person is re-born according to his past conduct. He may be a rich man or a poor man; he may be changed into an animal or a bird or an insect or a fish.'

Of all the answers it was the first that seemed most credible. But this brought me most despondency. 'Dead — finished!' What could be done about it? I had a poverty-stricken home and I was physically weak. It was my hope that my circumstances would improve and that eventually I could enjoy a little happiness. Even so at the end of 70 or 80 years at the most we would have to leave the world. Then it would be a case of 'Dead — finished!' There was nothing left. What a bitter prospect! I could not bring myself to accept its inevitability. I wanted to find a road to life. I cannot recall exactly how old I was when I began to turn these questions over in my mind. I know that it was before I began to go to school and certainly when I was between 6 and 9.

I had an uncle, my mother's elder brother, who was an honest and honourable man. He read many novels and his mind was full of stories. Every time he visited us I asked him to tell me a story. On one occasion I asked him, 'Uncle! Is there any way not to die?' He replied, 'Yes!' His reply brought me great comfort. I then asked him to tell me how to avoid death. He said, 'The way not to die is to go into the mountains and seek it. Get away from the world and its cares; give up fame and wealth; deny yourself all pleasure; meditate in a cave; drink the dew on the grass and on the leaves; and dig up fungus from the floor of your cave and eat it. By practising aceticism for a long time you will gradually become an immortal; you will not die.'

I was overjoyed to get this information. My hopes could be realized. I pleaded with my uncle to take me to the mountains to cultivate virtue. He said to me: 'Retiring to the mountains to seek the Way involves giving up all pleasure and turning from the wealth and fame of the world. Are you not loth to give up things like this?' I replied, 'I will give up everything. Whatever happens I must escape death. If there is indeed a way of avoiding death then show it to me and I will act accordingly'. But my uncle made excuses and evaded the issue. He was unwilling to take me to the mountains. I hoped that I would soon grow up and become a man, and I could then go by myself to the mountains and seek the Way. I nourished this hope in my heart, and for several years it brought me much comfort.

School days
I was probably about nine when my mother took me to the Tsui-Wun Lower Primary School established by the London Mission (London Missionary Society). My mother gave me a school name — Yong-Shung (Eternal Abundance); this was my third name. Apart from my baby name the name which my mother gave

me later was Deh-Shung (Virtue — Victory). So Yong-Shung was my third name. The school was situated inside the compound of the London Mission on Mi-Shih Street inside the Chong-Wun Gate. At that time the school had between 30 and 40 pupils and one teacher. Help in teaching was also given by the son of the teacher who was a medical student. We called him Elder Brother Teacher. A friend of this student also helped. The school was half old-style and half new-style. The curriculum included Arithmetic, History, Geography, Ethics, and Chinese Literature. The teacher, Mr. Yu, was between 50 and 60 years old. He strictly disciplined the pupils and all of them stood in awe of him. As soon as I entered the school I had to read the writings of Confucius. The teacher appreciated my progress and took pains to help me. I came top in every examination and the teacher nourished great hope for me. He was very excited about this and everywhere spoke in praise of his pupil. However, I became proud and slackened off in my studies, giving thought to nothing but play, so that my teacher became angry. One day he asked my mother to go to school and in front of me he said to her: 'Mrs Wong! This son of yours has great capabilities but of late he has not put his heart into his studies. I cannot bear to see him wasting his abilities in this way and I am going to discipline him more strictly. As his mother you must also discipline him in the home. If both of us attack this problem together we can ensure his making progress.' From then on I dare not slacken again.

The teacher in fact took great pains to help me, and expended great effort on my behalf. Alas! When I was at Higher Primary School two years later I heard the news of his passing. Since I was young I did not go to the funeral service but when I think of it, even now, I regret not having attended.

In my studies I read about the Emperor Chin-Shih and Han-Wu and how they sought the elixir of life without either of them finding it. Neither of them escaped death. I was plunged into the depths of despair. I had thought of these two emperors as being exalted men, as wealthy as the four seas, yet they were still unable to find the way of immortality. What hope had I — an ordinary human being? I made further enquiries of my uncle. He then acknowledged that he had been misleading me. What he had told me about retiring to the mountains to seek Truth and avoid death was all a joke. I could only relapse again into despondency. I feared death but knew that sooner or later I could not escape from it. I sought long life but had no means of ensuring it. I was pessimistic; I lost hope. No one could comfort me or bring me happiness. Whenever I gave myself to study or spent time in recreation my spirits would rise, but whenever I thought of human mortality I became conscious of bitter pain.

As already described, the circumstances of my childhood were particularly unhelpful. In middle life my mother had lost her husband; all she had was one girl and one boy (my sister and myself) and naturally we were as precious as two eyes. She was loth to punish us and discipline us so that we became overbearing in the extreme. She was elated that both of us did well in our studies and even less was she prepared to discipline us. How dangerous it is when a child is not disciplined!

A corrupt environment

I have mentioned the neighbours who rented the rooms in our courtyard. Five of them were living in one small room and three in another. Amongst these neighbours were food vendors, rickshaw pullers, barbers, cooks, messengers, and soldiers. Those best-off economically were only just able to maintain a reasonable existence. The most intelligent could only recognize a few (Chinese) characters. As for morality, the situation can be imagined. Lying, cursing, gambling, opium-smoking, stealing, fighting, sexual immorality and wicked practices of every kind. You name it – they did it.

One man who worked in the kitchen of a wealthy householder took home a basket, every evening, which was packed with rice, flour, oil, and meat from his employer's house. A man with three children pulled a rickshaw on the one hand and engaged in stealing on the other. One woman allowed a gambling group to meet in her house every evening and took a percentage of the winnings. One young woman, whenever her husband was absent, attracted various unprincipled men who cracked jokes and created disturbances in her room. A daughter-in-law took mean advantage of her mother-in-law. A depraved wife oppressed her husband making him kneel on the ground for long periods. Later on the same rooms were occupied by another couple when the situation was reversed – the husband beating his wife so severely that her whole body was covered with scars. A young wife lived alone in a small room, and every few days a well-dressed man would come and spend the night with her. Not for a long time did it come to light that she was a maid who acted as mistress to a rich young man. Another room was rented by a middle-aged man who kept the door locked most of the time but stayed there one or two days every week with a young woman. He announced that they were man and wife and that they worked away from home. But the man was arrested and charged with seduction. We then discovered that he was a clerk who rented the room to have clandestine meetings with his young girl cousin.

Thus during a period of more than 20 years we had all kinds of people living in our courtyard and all manner of incidents arose. This was the situation in which I grew up. We may say, in fact, that in our little courtyard was found a cross-section of Peking lower-class society. One is reminded of the mother of Mencius who moved her house many times through fear of her son being influenced and corrupted by his environment. If my own mother had followed this example, and allowed no questionable neighbours to move into our rooms, we as a family would have had nothing to eat.

When I was small I often went outside the court-yard to play — though I never ventured too far. Sometimes I would beg a copper or two from my mother so that I could go to the Eastern Peace Market Amusement Fair to watch the local theatricals. When I returned home I would get some black ink or red colouring and smear it on my face. Then I would take a wooden sword and jump around with excited cries or roll on the ground in the street.

There lived nearby at that time a well-to-do family. They had at least 20 servants, two or three four-wheeled carts, and five or six very big foreign horses. I frequently played with the carters. The unclean things that poured from their lips were atrocious.

When they saw me rolling on the ground they would shout 'Good!', and that only made me roll around even more excitedly, until I was quite exhausted. The people whom I came in contact with outside were exactly like those in the courtyard. My mother was busy with chores in the home — making clothes, doing the laundry and so on — and could never get round to controlling me. Rather than be hindered in her work she was content to let me play outside. Growing up as I did in an environment of impurity and wickedness like this, what hope did I have of being good?

Boarding School

When I was 12 I moved up from the Lower Primary to the Higher Primary, and I began to live at the school as a boarder. Academically I made some progress but in character I became much worse. There were 30 or 40 pupils altogether in the school. Amongst them were a few comparatively decent, but most of the older pupils took advantage of the younger pupils and the strong oppressed the weak. Some of the older pupils treated the younger ones as cruelly as masters treat slaves. Some of them taught the younger ones obscenities such as I had never heard even among our neighbours. I myself at that time had neither faith nor purpose, and I was carried along by the prevailing currents. If God had not manifested His amazing grace I truly cannot imagine to what depths of evil I would now have sunk.

Physically I was not too well and my strength was small. Whenever my fellow-pupils sprang into action it was invariably I who suffered. Yet I was able to open my mouth and bawl them out, and curse them. As a result I was often beaten. Nevertheless I never surrendered to brute force.

At that time I began to read novels extolling chivalry. I longed to become proficient in military arts so that in the future I would be strong enough to help the weak and to liberate the oppressed.

On one occasion the older pupils set out to cut off the hair of the younger pupils so that their heads were smooth. Within a few days all had their heads shaved smooth except me. In spite of their threats I refused to submit. Finally some of the older pupils became angry and decided to take action. 'If you don't have it shaved,' they said, 'we shall take a pair of scissors and cut off the hair on one side when you are sleeping.' 'All right' I replied, 'whoever dares to do this, I will take the scissors and stab his eyes.' As a consequence no-one made a move and my hair was preserved intact. It was I who claimed victory.

Development of Personality

Ever since I was small I have had a certain characteristic. No matter what issue arose unless I myself could see the rightness of a certain course of action, I would not blindly follow others. On the other hand, once I had seen the rightness of a certain course of action I would allow no obstacles to hinder me following it. I may be weak in body, but I am not weak in will. I have resisted people; I have resisted God. Yet while I have overcome many others it was God who overcame me. This is an experience which I will recount in detail later.

I am a mixture of two different natures. On the one hand I am conservative; on the other hand I am impulsive. In some things I am positively progressive. There are some things which in my view should never be changed; and that means not to change them even by a hair's breadth. There are other things which in my view ought to be changed; and that means to change them cleanly and completely. Because of the existence of these two natures I have given offence to many people during my progress from childhood to adulthood and this has meant bearing a considerable amount of bitterness. At the same time I have had considerable triumph and success.

Pupils who boarded at the school were only allowed to go outside from 12 noon until 6 o'clock on Saturdays. I always hurried home, where my mother had prepared many good things to eat. After eating I would rush off to the Eastern Peace Market to play. After another meal I would return to school. Unfortunately I always ate to excess, and my visits home were invariably followed by stomach-ache. I nevertheless maintained the same routine. My mother truly loved me. She herself was always unwilling to eat good things or to wear nice clothes, but she always gave these things to her children. My mother really spoilt us. I urge mothers who love their children not to spoil them. Even more I urge children to remember the love of their parents. My mother is no longer living, but I still want to do things for her so that she may get some pleasure. Yet the opportunity has gone. To write this is enough to make me weep. Those of you who have parents, do your best to respect them now. Do not wait until a day when you sigh in vain 'The tree wants peace but the wind does not cease; the child wants to care but the parents are deceased.'

Conditions were bad in the courtyard at home; they were also bad at school. No one at home could teach me how to act as a man; no one at school could teach me this either. The teacher at school only

17

encouraged pupils to study to the best of their ability. Although the curriculum included 'Ethics', we studied it in the same way that we studied Chinese Literature. We did not cultivate our characters. There was a teacher who paid attention to the cleanliness and neatness of our uniform, and who taught us the etiquette to follow when we had an interview with the school-master. After breakfast every morning all the pupils paraded and attended morning chapel. The teacher stood at the entrance to check that faces were washed and uniforms buttoned. In the winter my hands were invariably chapped and I was afraid to wash my hands and face. One morning the teacher noticed me and reproved me: 'Yong-Shung! With mud like that on the back of your neck you can soon sow wheat. Quickly go back and wash.' I returned shamefacedly and washed myself absolutely clean. From that day on I made sure that my face and my hands were washed properly. The same teacher also taught us that whenever we met the school-master we should stand respectfully and bow. Of the good training which I received when I was young it is this that remains. Even now whenever I encounter a former supervisor I stand and bow in this way. But other lessons such as how to act as becomes a man I did not learn until, at the age of 14, I believed in the Lord.

False Christianity

When I was young I was regularly taken to church by my mother — my parents being members of the London Mission. At school I attended a worship service every day. When I became a boarder the opportunities to attend such services increased. Every day in the week, from Monday to Saturday, all the pupils in the two schools — Boys' and Girls' — went to chapel in the morning for half-an-hour's service. Every Wednesday afternoon there was a Prayer Meeting. Each Sunday morning brought Sunday School and the main service of worship. Christian Endeavour was held in the afternoon and a meeting for young people in the evening. In addition to these services Bible classes were held three or four times each week. Chapel services were compulsory.

Examinations were held for Bible classes as for other subjects and marks were awarded. In order to accumulate marks the pupils mechanically memorized Bible passages, but after the examinations were over they had no further interest in these passages. Moreover, all the passages we studied were from the historical parts of the Bible. Doctrinal truths were never studied. Chapel attendance was compulsory but we were never examined on what we heard. As a result many pupils used the opportunity to prepare their lessons; others secretly read novels; still others would go to sleep. In any case the sermons were both uninteresting and powerless.

In term time the chapel was invariably full, seven or eight tenths being pupils, but as soon as we came to the summer holiday or to New Year holiday the attendance of pupils faded away like the morning star.

To sum up, from the time when my intelligence blossomed, to my 14th year I passed my life chaotically, unintelligibly, confusedly, without faith, without purpose, without hope, and without a clear track. I could find neither an illuminated road nor a leader to direct me. Apart from my academic achievements and the wilfulness in my disposition I in no way differed from others. I nourished evil thoughts and employed evil language. I did not commit any blatant sin. For one thing I was still young and for another I had never had much courage. I was thin-skinned and greatly feared to lose face. The fact of our family being poverty-stricken was an advantage in that there are many sins you cannot commit without money. If I had not repented and believed for another 10 years or 20 years I do not know to what degree my life would have been corrupted.

Conversion

I was 14 when God saved me. In the spring of that year an older fellow-student in the school sought me

out to talk with me. For a long time I had been deeply impressed by his character and by his love, so when he came to talk with me I readily received him. He led me to know God; he also showed me how to worship God. He also showed me how to pray, how to read the Bible, how to examine myself daily, and also how to keep a diary. He gave me a book edited by H.L. Zia entitled 'A Help to Personal Development' from which I received tremendous help. I continued to read other books written or translated by Mr Zia. My life and my attitudes were vastly changed. I began to understand the meaning of life and its responsibilities. I began to hate all sin and unrighteousness. I began to long for a life of purity and goodness. I became interested in prayer and Bible-reading. I became unhappy about my unsatisfactory manner of life. I hated all the wicked things I had said to my fellow-pupils and all the wicked things I had done. I began to attend meetings in the chapel voluntarily, and at Easter I was baptized in the chapel. I then considered myself a proper Christian. And I resolved to be a good Christian. The schoolmate who had led me to the Lord was a great help to me. For one thing he never hesitated to reprove me severely whenever he saw me in the wrong. This made me love him all the more. At the same time I was in awe of him. In the summer I graduated from Higher Primary School and moved up to the first year class in the Middle School. That year my friend was in the 4th year of the Middle School so we had one year together there. In 1915 he graduated and we had to separate.

I was clearly aware of the change that had taken place in me but I did not understand what it was all about. Previously I had given expression to all sorts of bad language and engaged in all sorts of evil conduct without any sorrow or any sense of shame whatever, but after that year I was completely different. If I ever used evil words I was conscious of pain and self-reproof in my heart. I often beat my chest with my fists. I wept many tears over my sin and I uttered many sighs. I often confessed my sin to God. I made many resolutions and I experienced many failures. I fell and I got up again; I got up and I fell again. Sometimes I overcame temptation which made me elated and pleased; at other times it was temptation which overcame me and I was disappointed and grieved. I knew I was not good but I wanted to be good; but although I wanted to be good I lacked the power to be good. My experience was bitter in the extreme. From one point of view I now had faith, I had purpose, and I had the will to climb higher. I had no wish to pass my days stupidly and worthlessly, and this was a good phenomenon, but from another point of view there was still conflict within my heart, and I felt the opposing influences of good and evil.

While the school-mate who led me to the Lord was still at school he continued to rebuke and restrain me, and I was very pleased that he did so, but when he left the school my circumstances were very different. I repeatedly reproved myself and hated myself but this seemed to have little effect. I wished that my friend could return to help me, but this, of course, was out of the question. However, I thank God that He completed His work in me through other people. These people, however, were not my friends. They were my enemies and they did not like me. The story is as follows.

Persecution
During my second year at Middle School the school

admitted some new students from wealthy families. The father of one pupil was an official; the father of another was an important merchant. Because of their background they were in a position to spend money lavishly; their conduct, however, was depraved and dissolute. All day long their mouths were full of obscene expressions and evil talk. They exerted an evil influence on other students. I was pained and indignant at all I saw and heard, but they were all my fellow-students and no one had authority to restrain them. The time came, however, when I could no longer remain silent, and I went to talk to a responsible teacher. Since our headmaster lived at Tung-Hsien, and only came to the school once or twice each week, the affairs of the school were left in the hands of this teacher. I begged him to think of a way to restrain these students and I was totally unprepared for his reply. 'In order to maintain the income of the school' he said, 'we cannot be too conscientious regarding the conduct of these students. For if we expel all the students who are depraved we shall lose the school fees and in that case how shall we maintain the school?' I was filled with indignation. I then engaged in noisy argument with the teacher. (I was so zealous for the Lord at that time it made me bold). I said: 'Rather than run a school that corrupts children in this way it would be better to close the school as quickly as possible.' I also said, 'For believers in Christ to run a school and to tolerate evil practices on the part of students in this way is to abandon Christian principles.' I was not aware that one of the depraved students had also come to see the teacher. He did not come into the room but he heard all that I had said. He informed the others in the group and from that time on they hated me 'to the bone' and ceaselessly sought means of getting their own back.

They did all they could to search out my wrongdoings. They called me all kinds of names. They called me 'Dr Morality' and 'Pharisee'. If I ever said a word out of place or did anything wrong they would attack me, pointing at me and saying, 'Does not Dr Morality do the same things as publicans and sinners?' They used all means possible of reviling me and attacking me. I had enemies all round me; it was a very bitter experience. Yet the Lord used these wicked enemies of mine to keep me straight. Before I left the Middle School the school moved to new quarters and the headmaster also moved from Tung-Hsien. He exercised far greater control than there had been before. Of those in that group of depraved students some were severely punished, some were expelled, some withdrew on their own initiative. Because of the attacks of these enemies my own life was gradually brought on to the track, and before I graduated I became a more presentable youth. It was their intention to harm me, but God used them to complete His work in me. God's acts are truly amazing.

Spiritual Help

Apart from getting help from the student who led me to the Lord as I have already mentioned I was greatly helped at that time by one whom I had never met, Mr Zia of the Young Men's Christian Association. From the time I read 'A Help to Personal Development' I bent every effort to acquire all the books that he had translated or edited. In the nurture of a young Christian they were immensely helpful. You can understand from his writings why he was loved and respected. The help which I received from him can never be measured. Alas! Not only did I never meet him, I never even wrote him a letter. When the news came through that Mr Zia had died I was as saddened as if I had lost a close relative. When I went later to Hangchow (in June 1925) I visited Mr Zia's grave and saw his gravestone. This gracious teacher was never aware that I was one of his students. The fact that I now pay special attention to the practical life of a Christian as I do is probably because I have been greatly influenced by Mr Zia. Alas, the YMCA today no longer publishes books like those that were written or translated by Mr Zia.

2.
Separated from my Mother's womb...

Then the word of the Lord came unto me saying 'Before I formed thee in the belly I knew thee; and before thou camest forth out of the womb I sanctified thee, and I ordained thee a prophet unto the nations.

(Jeremiah 1:4,5)

But when it pleased God, who separated me from my mother's womb, and called me by His grace to reveal His Son in me, that I might preach Him among the heathen; immediately I conferred not with flesh and blood.

(Galatians 1:15,16)

The prophet Jeremiah and the apostle Paul both knew that God had separated them from their mother's womb. Reflecting on the experiences of half a life-time I know that I have not only been clearly commissioned as God's servant but that I too have been separated by God from my mother's womb. From my infancy I have always been physically weak and only rarely has a full year passed without my being ill. When I was at school a term hardly passed without my being absent on account of illness. Before I reached the age of eighteen I was seriously ill on four or five occasions. First, at the age of 3 or 4 I became seriously ill with dysentery and for a number of days was a patient in the London Mission Hospital. I was so ill that the doctor said to my mother, 'There is no longer any hope for the child.' My mother and my grandmother both advocated that I should be taken home immediately. The thought in their minds was this: since he cannot recover then let him die at home and on no account let him die in hospital. I still have a vague memory of being carried by my grandmother in a sedan chair and taken home. Strangely, once I got home I gradually recovered.

At the age of 8 or 9 I again became seriously ill. I suffered from an exceedingly painful swelling in the head. I was taken to several hospitals but none of the doctors could do anything for me. Finally I was kept in hospital. My mother was not really happy about this but because it was the only way she finally stayed with me in the hospital. Still the disease showed no sign of clearing up and everyone became anxious. My mother was afraid for my life. Again, strangely, one day there was a copious discharge from my ear and from that time on I gradually recovered. My next serious illness was at the age of fifteen when I had a high temperature and was unable to eat anything for many days. My mother had no medical knowledge and all that she could do was to watch over me. The illness worsened and then, again strangely, began to

27

pass. Another illness, at the age of eighteen, was even more serious, but God again acted miraculously and preserved my life.

Looking back I realize that any of these illnesses could have proved fatal. The poverty-stricken circumstances of my childhood together with my mother's ignorance of medical care would have compounded the danger. Had it not been for God having chosen me and preserved me I truly do not know how I could have survived until the present.

Strength given

If you knew of my weakness as a child and of my tendency to illness you would certainly never believe that I could be involved in the complicated work I do today. People observe that I often preach twice a day, and when this includes leading the singing (which means about two hours each session) they would never realize that as a child I was weak and ailing. I am myself amazed at the abundant energy I possess and acknowledge that it is purely because God has called and commissioned me.

There is another feature which speaks of the special grace of God. No matter where I go — from the northern part of our country to the south, from the eastern part to the west; no matter what climates I work in — whether in the north and north-east where the temperature drops to 30 or 40 degrees below zero, or in Fujien and Gwongdong at the height of summer; no matter what food I eat — whether the wheat-flour of the north or the rice of the south or the sorghum of Manchuria, whether Chinese style or Western style — my physical well-being has never been adversely affected in any way. Soft water, hard water, insipid water, brackish water — none of this upset my digestion. When it comes to travel — apart from being sick on board ship in rough seas — I am never conscious of discomfort no matter what the means of travel. There are those who cannot sleep when they first move to a new locality but my ministry has never been hindered by this.

Further, God caused me to be born and brought up in Peking and to speak the national language freely. This was also God's special preparation, for the national language is everywhere current and generally understood. This factor has had a large bearing on my work of preaching. Some say that I am eloquent, but what they say is incorrect. My associates can testify that in ordinary conversation I am neither fluent nor clever; in fact I sometimes betray a slight stammer. Most of all I am aware of inability, through the use of inappropriate language, to clear up misunderstandings. I could even cause the breach to be widened. When I am speaking in the ordinary way, apart from enunciating clearly and using a resonant voice, my speech has no particular excellence, but when it comes to preaching it is as if my mouth and tongue are transformed. I realize from this that eloquence and gift are two completely different things. God's gift is naturally dependent on God's call.

Literature is not my forte. Poetry, songs, verse, stories — not one of these have I studied. Not one of them can I compose. Yet God enables me with simple phraseology to testify to the truth. Some people speak of what they call 'a stomach manuscript'. This refers to a composition formed in the mind before the writer takes up a pen to start writing. I have never been able to compose 'a stomach manuscript'. However, when I have an inspiration I take up a pen and start writing. As I write, the ideas follow one another in succession. It is the same with my preaching. The method of some preachers is to sit down for several hours and turn up this book and that, to take pen and paper and prepare a manuscript, and then when the time comes to mount the pulpit and preach. That is a procedure I rarely follow. When I preach I first get a message from God: I then take this message with me into the pulpit. I use Scripture passages well known to me and I deal with facts and principles with which I am familiar; in this way I transmit the message to the congregation. The language I use is plain and forthright and true. If God withdraws His gift I immediately lose my power and become a nobody.

All that God does is wonderful. He delivered me from the deep pit of sin; He cleansed me through the blood of His Son our Lord Jesus Christ, and by His Spirit He gave a new birth and I became His child. He also chose me and called me, bringing me into His Service and setting me up to be a watchman both in the world and in the church. He commanded me to labour for the Gospel, to battle for His Truth, and to witness to His Way. When I reflect on these things I cannot doubt His call in the slightest and I dare not have even the appearance of idleness.

Ambition

I was fifteen when God began to call me. Previous to that I had nourished a great ambition to become a great politician. That was my ideal. In the autumn of the year when I became fourteen I was strolling one evening with the student who had led me to the Lord. He asked me out of the blue what I had made up my mind to do in the future. I was still young at that time and I had not given thought to that question, so I could not answer him. I simply said that really I had no particular inclination and that I would go where the fancy took me. 'That' he said 'will not do.' He told me that a young man must have a purpose and he quoted the teaching of the sage, 'It is the purposeful who gain success.' He urged me to make up my mind and I naturally wanted to follow his suggestion. I began to think about the matter. I thought again about the end of human life. My friend had led me to worship God and to believe in the Lord Jesus, but he had not helped me clearly to understand the grace of God and His promises about the future life. I feared death and was unwilling to think about life after death. I had failed in my quest for immortality. The next best thing was to carry out some great enterprise so that when I died I would leave behind a famous name. As the saying goes, 'When a fox dies it leaves a skin; when a man dies he leaves a reputation.' The question had arisen, What should I engage in to obtain the greatest fame? I finally decided to become a politician. This was because I learned from history and also from newspapers that the fame of politicians was far greater than that of people in any other walk of life.

However, I had realized after a while that I lacked the means to become a politician. My background was one of poverty and I lacked influence. I had no eminent relatives or friends with rank who could help me to climb on to the political stage. My ambition suffered a shock. However, before long I read about the American President Abraham Lincoln and I learned that his original background had been one of poverty and obscurity like my own. If he could become a great politician, why should not I? Lincoln became my hero. I bought his picture and put it on the wall. I zealously believed in the Lord but I applied myself to study with the purpose of becoming eventually a great politician.

Calling

It was in the autumn of the year in which I became 14 that I made up my mind to be a politician. At the beginning of the year following I began to be conscious of God's call for me to be a preacher. When the summons first came I resisted it. How could I be a preacher when my mind was set on becoming a politician? Becoming a great politician was a matter for glory whereas becoming a preacher was a matter of debasement. To throw over my ambition to be a politician in order to become a preacher was like descending from a lofty tree into a dark ravine. There was another reason for my reluctance. I had come across a lot of preachers who were worthless. Some of them had originally been language teachers for the missionaries and had gradually evolved into preachers. Some of them had served the missionaries as cooks, cleaners, gatemen and so on; they heard preaching all the time, they learned a few passages of scripture, they sang a few hymns and went on to preach a few half-understood doctrines. They moved on from this to be regular preachers. Others had failed to make the grade in ordinary schools or colleges and all that remained was to go to Bible School for two years. Then they would go into the church as preachers.

I flattered myself that I myself was not that kind of worthless student. My name was frequently listed among the prize-winners and this brought financial help for my school fees. For a person so endowed and so gifted to become a preacher was, in my view, for a talented person to serve in an inferior capacity. I therefore steadfastly rejected God's call.

I was however a young man zealously believing in the Lord. Every morning after rising and every evening before retiring I prayed without fail. I read the Bible at least once every day. I never missed the regular services of worship. In term time, of course, attendance was compulsory, but I made a point of attending also in the holidays when most of the seats were empty. I was not conscious of being greatly benefitted by these services but I recognized that a good Christian would on no account give up his church attendance. I also attended the young people's meetings and shared in their activities. I would be seen as a most zealous Christian. Naturally the more zealous I became the more clearly was I conscious that He was calling me to be a preacher for Him. Nevertheless I still backed away, and I still made excuses. It was as if, out of a hundred of God's commands, I was willing to obey ninety-nine. It was just this one that I had no means of obeying. To give up my ambition to be a politician and to become a preacher was a proposition that I could on no account accept.

Conflict

For a period of over three years, from the age of 15 to 18, I was engaged in a controversy with God. The struggle was extremely painful to me. Yet I did not give way, and neither did God. Sometimes I shut out from my mind all thoughts of the future, and temporarily my heart was at peace. Yet whenever I thought about the matter the conflict was revived.

On one occasion the school arranged special meetings, with an enthusiastic speaker, which lasted several days. 'Young Christians,' said the speaker, 'should make up their minds to be preachers.' As I was regarded as the most zealous student in the school — and as in any case attendance was compulsory — I could not stay away, though I sought an excuse to do so. As a result of all this the struggle in my heart blazed up afresh.

In the summer of the year in which I became 18 I should graduate from Middle School (it was still the old Middle School system of 4 years). Before entering university I would need to choose the subjects I wanted to study. I could no longer delay. In view of my ambition to be a politician I made up my mind to study politics. On my breast I wore the slogan 'Human determination will decide destiny.' I was quite confident that if I decided to become a politician I could certainly become one. I was using my own stubbornness to deal with God. I was acting stupidly, like 'taking an egg to strike a stone.'

Submission
In the middle of March that year (1918) I became ill. My body was tired, my head was dizzy, and I had to take to my bed with a temperature. I had no appetite. The illness lasted more than a month before it cleared up. Early in May I returned to school but on May 20th I became ill again. On 23rd I had to return home. The disease got worse; but I forced myself to sit for an examination for Middle School students in Mission Schools in the two provinces Hobeh and Shansi. The examination lasted 5 days but after 2 days I had to go to bed again. When the illness was at its worst I began to think that I would not recover; I feared death. I lost hope. I then regretted that I had resisted the call of God. I

reached the point where there was no other way than
to abandon my ambition to be a politician. I now
realized that I could not prevail against God. 'Human
determination will decide destiny' was the statement
of a lunatic. Caught between pain on the one hand
and despair on the other I made my silent prayer to
God. I confessed that I ought to die but I promised
God that if He would preserve my life I would not
dare again to stand out against Him. I had taken a lot
of medicine but it seemed to have no effect whatever.
A doctor at the London Mission Hospital told my
sister that there was no hope of my disease being

cured. But then the unexpected happened. When my unspoken prayer reached God's ear He marvellously healed what was a very serious illness.

Thus it happened that God used these two occasions of serious illness to compel my submission and to do away with my ambition to be a politician. I finally recovered at the end of June. On June 27th the graduation ceremony took place at the school. Because my results up to then had been good the school allowed me to graduate like the rest. I had now completed my four years of study at Middle School.

University

I was still physically weak and my friends urged me to take a complete rest. But I was unwilling to hinder my studies further and in mid-September I resumed my studies. At that time the Middle School Course was four years and the university course six years. The first two years of the latter were for the Preparatory Course and the remaining four years for the Regular Course. At that time I was a first-year student in the Preparatory Course.

Home ties

On May 19th 1919 all schools went on strike on account of national events. We engaged in no more studies that term and on June 3rd we broke up early for the summer vacation. I then received a notice saying that first-year students taking the Preparatory Course would be transferred in the autumn to Cheloo University at Jinan in Shandong Province. I was very uneasy about this since I had never before travelled so far. In addition, my mother and I were very close and during the years I boarded in Peking I had gone home regularly once a week. My mother needed to see me frequently and I needed to see her frequently. Were I to go to Jinan we would not meet for at least half a year. We could not be separated for so long, particularly since she was often unwell and was ill at the time in question. I recalled a time when my mother had been ill the previous year (1918). Monday, September 30th, was a half-day's holiday and I went home from school in high spirits. But on entering the door I found my mother ill in bed and my spirits drooped immediately. I hastily sent a telegram calling home my sister (a school teacher). I was required by school regulations to be back at school that evening so there was no alternative to asking my sister to stay overnight. But the next day was the birthday of Confucius and this meant a whole day's holiday, so I was again free to go home and look after my mother. I still had to be back at school that evening, and my sister had already gone back, so we were in a dilemma. I was extremely worried and wept many tears. At half past eight I had to go back to school. On the following day although my body was in the classroom my heart was at home, and I was wondering all the time whether my mother was worse. Other students listened to the lectures but I could only sit weeping with my head bowed. I finally got permission to return home after lessons for a period of several days. My mother then recovered.

But it was only a matter of days before my mother and sister became ill at the same time. How could I relax at school? I needed to go home after school to look after them but I dare not ask permission to be away again so soon. I stuck it out until the evening meal but I could not bear it any longer. I slipped out of the school gate unobtrusively after lessons and returned in the evening. From the time that I had believed in the Lord I had been unwilling to infringe school regulations. But on this occasion I repeated my visits home until both my mother and sister were well again.

The anxiety of those days, however, had a physical effect on me. I was tired and unable to eat properly. I did not sleep soundly and constantly bathed my face in tears. My body and my mind were both under attack. So as soon as my mother and sister were better, after three days, I myself became ill for another ten days. I was given leave to go home to recuperate and I was looked after by my mother. We were inseparable. How could I go to Jinan several hundred miles away?

Plans for the future

Throughout the period from June to August I passed through many days of anxiety. It was in my mind that when I had completed the two years of the Preparatory Course I would take the examination for the Regular Course. So I went to see Principal Chin of my mother school enquiring whether he would permit me to take this examination. Principal Chin advised me to see the Department Head of the Regular Course (seemingly a missionary) and to discuss the matter with him. But contrary to all expectations, although I called many times, from beginning to end I never got to see him. I wrote a letter but not even a postcard came in reply. While hope faded that I would ever get the necessary permission, I hoped at least for a reply, saying 'Yes' or 'No', so that my heart could be at rest. Alas! Not even a couple of words were given in reply. I was frustrated and angry. It had never even occurred to me that a western missionary who had come in the name of Christ 'from a distance across many seas' in order to serve the Chinese church could treat a young and ambitious Chinese student like this.

My hope of taking the Regular Course had now gone. I still could not bear the thought of leaving my mother to go to Jinan. Now that my hope of entering university had been summarily ended I wanted to take my own life. I almost became mentally ill. Thank God in the days of darkness and pain He used His own words to comfort me. On the morning of the 22nd I was helped by my Scripture reading: 'Whether we live, we live unto the Lord; and whether we die, we die unto the Lord: whether we live therefore, or die, we are the Lord's' (Romans 14:8). Then on the morning of the 23rd I got these promises from God, 'With everlasting kindness will I have mercy on thee . . my kindness shall not depart from thee.' (Isaiah 54:8,10).

Since the door for further study was now closed I had to find a temporary job and try for higher education later. On the surface it should not be difficult to get employment, for most of those who knew me at that time would hold me in high regard. It was a strange thing, however, that no matter how I tried I could not find a place anywhere. Before we knew it, we had reached the end of August. I could see no glimmer of light whatever. I was depressed and in despair.

An Open Door
On the evening of August 26th I went to the home

of my friend (the one who had led me to the Lord). He exhorted me not to grieve over the situation and urged me to go away for a change of environment. He urged me to go to Tung-Hsien and travel around for a day or two. Just at that time the Board of Education of the Christian churches (presumably of the denomination) in the two provinces Hobeh and Shansi was meeting in Tung-Hsien and I would meet not a few people known to me. Because of my circumstances I did not particularly want to meet people and was not keen on going. But he strongly urged me to do so and thus, on the following day, I left for Tung-Hsien. I stayed only a day and a half until the meetings were concluded. I then returned with others to Peking. But in an unexpected way it was through my stay in Tung-Hsien that I found a way out. It happened as follows:

While in Tung-Hsien I met a friend whom I had not seen for three or four years. When he heard that I had not yet found anything to do he introduced me to a Primary School in Baoding where there was a vacancy for a teacher. The work involved teaching pupils in the Lower Primary School and the salary for a married teacher was $ 12 a month, that for unmarried teachers being 80% of that. I did not consider this work altogether suitable and my reaction was to decline it. But my friend urged me to think about it. 'Today is the 28th' he said, 'They will await your reply until the end of the month. At the latest, please give them a reply on the 31st.' I agreed to do this. But although I thought about it for several days I still felt that I couldn't accept it. I could not go away as a student to Jinan (more than 300 miles) and how could I go as a teacher to Bao-ding (100 miles)? In addition to that, teaching Primary School pupils was not my line. I had given some help in teaching pupils in Tsui-Wun Primary

School while I was a second year student in Middle School. But I had now studied for one year at university and I was also a purposeful young man with hopes of achieving something important. How could I lower my sights to the point of teaching Primary School pupils? In the third place I felt that the salary was very inadequate. I should need to return home at least once a month and each trip would cost $ 14. I would find it difficult to make ends meet. There would certainly be nothing available to buy books and clothing; still less would I be able to save anything. No, I could not accept it. So on the evening of August 31st I wrote a letter saying that I could not go to Baoding. I then went out to post the letter.

On reaching the pillar box I put the letter in the aperture, but before I released it I glanced at the list of collection times which I could see in the light of the street lamp. I then observed the notice, 'Next collection 7 a.m.' What should I do? I had promised to reply not later than the 31st. Now it was too late for the last collection that day. Rather than let the letter lie all night in the pillar box I had better take it home and post it the next morning. In rather low spirits I went home. That night I could only sigh in my sadness. Why is it, I thought, that my situation is so miserable? The door is closed to further study. I find a vacancy for a job but it is unsuitable. Why is God treating me like this? But the following morning my thinking suddenly changed. I decided to take the path that repelled me. Going to Baoding was certainly better than being at home in misery. So I tore up the letter I had written the night before and wrote another letter to Baoding accepting their invitation.

School Teaching

I left Peking on September 11th. My mother shed tears at the thought of my going so far away. Naturally, I cried as well. I was met at Baoding and taken to the school in the Gospel Courtyard in the west suburb.

On entering the school courtyard I observed the small rooms and the young pupils in their country style of dress. It fell short of my expectations. I felt intensely lonely and mournful. When I met the Principal he said that because the one who introduced me had mentioned my knowledge and experience he had decided to allocate a Higher Primary teacher to teach Lower Primary and for me to teach pupils of two classes — Higher Primary and First year Middle School pupils. In other words, the highest classes in the school. Also he would treat me with favour and allow me the salary of a married teacher. I was greatly encouraged by these arrangements, particularly those relating to teaching. I began teaching the next day, and after lessons were over I sought to help the pupils with Bible doctrine.

I recollected how I had been helped as a student by the writings of Pastor H.L. Zia whose intellectual standing and moral standards I greatly admired. I noted how he taught and guided the students, how he communicated with them and associated with them, and how through his own upright conduct he influenced them. I had thought at the time that if ever I became a teacher I would follow the pattern of Pastor Zia. So when I became a teacher in Baoding I sought to do this both inside the classroom and also outside the classroom. I explained to the pupils the great themes of worshipping God and living as becomes a man. What I preached at that time was very different from what I preach now. I did not then understand the doctrine of salvation and of life; I simply taught the students to worship God, to love men, and to live moral upright lives. I acted out of sincerity and zeal so I was well able to influence the pupils. At first these classes were after ordinary lessons had finished. But later I felt that it was better to have a meeting every day so that those pupils who wished to hear the message could attend voluntarily. I discussed the matter with some of the students and we arranged to have a prayer meeting every evening.

Counselling

We held the first meeting on November 12th. From that day on, apart from occasions when either the church or the school held a meeting, or when some other special circumstance arose, we met in this way every evening. Sometimes I talked to the students about prayer or Bible reading, sometimes I talked about making progress in moral living, sometimes about confession of sin and repentance, sometimes about practical life and how to live as becomes a man, sometimes about service and sacrifice, sometimes about hygiene and care of the body, sometimes about honouring one's parents, sometimes about honesty and holiness, sometimes about ruling one's family and saving the nation, sometimes about denying self and loving others, sometimes about virtue and wisdom, about maxims and mottoes, and sometimes about the biographies of famous people. But I could not at that time preach about the doctrine of life. It was not that I did not believe it but that I did not clearly comprehend it. I knew that Jesus atoned for my sin and died in my place. I also knew that apart from Jesus no one could come into the presence of God. As for the future life I did not fully understand it so I did not preach about it. I believed that all the records in the Bible were true, though I was only interested in the precious familiar passages. I believed that Jesus rose from the dead but I did not understand whether his body was raised or not. I believed in the miracles performed by the Lord Jesus and the prophets and the apostles as recorded. But when some people distorted the sense of these historical facts I could not distinguish truth from error. I remembered that when I was a Middle School student an elderly lady once preached to us on the subject of the Lord's Return, and I firmly believed the promises. But from that time on I rarely heard anyone preach on the subject and paid little attention.

Hostility

Apart from teaching the students I sought to nurture them in every way. A few students were much affected and they received my teaching. However, I encountered hostility from my colleagues. The first reason for this was that I did not live with them. Every day we five teachers ate together in one small room. When the other four talked among themselves they invariably found pleasure in lewd conversation and wild statements. I was greatly irritated (pricked in the ear as we say) by this. But they were all long-standing teachers whereas I was a newcomer. In addition I was much younger than them so I had no means of interfering. All that I could do when they engaged in this kind of talk was to remain silent, and to bow my head while eating my food. I was not accustomed to hearing conversation like that and I was embarrassed. My displeasure was plain to see and it called forth their hatred and hostility. On one occasion I could not bear to continue listening and I left my seat and went indignantly out.

After a further period I could bear it no longer and proposed that I should eat by myself in my own room. I had adequate reasons to do this since at that time I was a vegetarian (I did this for one and a half years). So I said to them: 'Since we do not eat the same kind of food there is no need for us to eat in the same place; it is better for me to eat by myself in my own room.'

There was another reason for my colleagues being resentful towards me. It was envy. In the ordinary way teachers taught only those subjects that they were obliged to teach. Other matters concerning the school or the students held no interest for them. Questions arising in the school were dealt with by a teacher responsible for them, and more important matters were dealt with by the Principal (at that time the school had no Principal and an elderly Western missionary had temporarily taken the position). Should any disorder arise among the students, unless the teacher responsible appointed other teachers to act for him, no one would show any interest. At that time I was extremely zealous and I did not enquire whether or not anyone had appointed me to act. Whenever I saw anything that needed to be done then I stepped forward to do it. In this way the teacher responsible acquired an active helper and he was very delighted. But the other teachers despised me and accused me of showing off my diligence to curry favour with the Principal. Most of all they misunderstood my association with the students and my arranging meetings for them. They did not appreciate that I was seeking to use the Truth as a means of nurturing the students' minds. They regarded my association with the students as a means of establishing my authority. So they maligned me and attacked me in every possible way. Sometimes, because of this, I lost heart and became despondent. But as soon as I saw the students anxious to be instructed then my heart was lifted up.

A Godly influence

One Sunday, after the mid-day meal, I saw two students clashing with each other. It so happened that the responsible teacher was not in the school, so I called the students to my room and asked them what it was all about. The younger student said, 'He hit me.'

The older one countered: 'He cursed me.' I let them both sit down. Then I began to exhort them and told them a very moving story (it was a story that had influenced me). As I talked I watched their faces. I noticed that they were truly moved. So after I had finished talking I asked them to state their case again. Unexpectedly the younger student stood up and said, 'Teacher, the affair was my fault because I first cursed him and that was why he hit me.' The older student also stood up and said, 'Teacher, the fault was mine. No matter what, I am older than he is so I ought not to strike him.' Seeing that, I urged them to shake hands and be reconciled. They had come weeping and quarrelling into my study, and now, an hour later, they went out talking and joking. Moreover from that day on the younger one was vastly changed.

After working for several months among students my thinking underwent a great transformation. Originally I had set my heart on becoming an influential politician. Although on account of a serious illness when I was 18 I had had to abandon my ambition I had still been unable to accept happily the will of God. But I now began to look at preaching in a new light and saw it as a great and important work. Even the president of a country could not change people's hearts so that they would turn their back on evil and move towards righteousness. Amongst the students I had been discussing Truth for several months and the lives of some of them had been remarkably changed. How can you estimate the value of work like this? Previously I had resisted God's call to me. But through my work of teaching I was beginning to set my heart on the work of God.

Apart from this there was now another reason for

my being ready to consider the work of God. During
the year in which I had studied in the Preparatory
Course at university I had on several occasions seen
people turning their back on the Truth. I had seen
instances of lying and deceit; of gaining profit for
oneself while causing loss to others; of the strong
insulting the weak; of toadying to the rich and
despising the poor. I began to discover that all kinds
of sinful practices in society had their exact counter-
parts in the church. I saw much in Baoding that made

me unhappy. I became much more aware of the darkness and corruption in the churches. I felt strongly that the church needed a revolution and that the mission to bring about a revolution was entrusted to me. This made me now willing to devote my life to the work of God.

The call obeyed

By the spring of 1920 I had unconditionally submitted to God and was now willing to respond to His call. It was in the summer of that year that I formally changed my name. My personal name was now 'Ming-dao' instead of 'Yong-shung'. The meaning enshrined in this name is as follows: May God use me in this world of darkness and depravity to testify to His truth.' The 'ming' here has the meaning of testify (certify) and it is not the 'ming' of understand. ('Dao' means a road, a way. Also the Way; the Truth. A doctrine).

The general level or morality gets lower and lower. What the world needs today is a man of virtue, power and determination, who will devote himself to the transformation of the human heart. Yesterday when we were studying in class the history of England our teacher Mr Hsu said to us, 'China is in urgent need of a man like John Wesley. Who is John Wesley? It may be there is one right in this class!' Ah! Is there such a one? I think it over and I think it over again. And I can only answer, 'There is!'

Now that I had accepted the call of God I prepared myself to continue study at university and then to study at a Theological College. The Principal, an Englishman, Mr Thomas Biggin, had once made a proposition to me. When he returned to his country he would if possible raise money for a grant that would enable me, some time in the future, to study in

England. This greatly excited me. I reckoned that I could first study four years at university and three years in the theological department of a university in China. After that I could go to England and study three years at a Theological College there. Thus after 10 years I would be a great pastor, a great evangelist.

But this was not the path that God had planned for me. 'My thoughts' He said, 'are not your thoughts, neither are your ways my ways . . . For as the heavens are higher than the earth, so are my ways higher than your ways, and my thoughts than your thoughts' (Isaiah 55:8,9). The path He planned for me was greatly superior. Because there was still a question about my entering university I decided, after praying over the matter for many days, to accept the invitation to continue teaching for another year. So early in September I again left Peking to resume teaching in Baoding.

Who could imagine that before the end of that term God would do a wonderful thing for me? He not only directed me along a different path; He also completely changed my thinking, my faith, and my life.

3.
Through fire and through water into a wealthy place...

Psalm 66:1-12
'For Thou, O God, hast proved us: Thou hast tried us, as silver is tried. Thou broughtest us into the net; thou laidest affliction upon our loins. Thou hast caused men to ride over our heads; we went through fire and through water; but Thou broughtest us out into a wealthy place.'
(Psalm 66:10-12).

When silver is refined in the fire it does not experience pain because it has no feeling. But when people are refined it means pain indescribable. Yet unless you are refined in that way your life will not be purified and enriched like unadulterated silver. How does God test us? And how does He discipline us? He brings us into the net. He lays burdens on our backs. He allows chariots to crush our heads. Not one of these three experiences is easy to endure. We can imagine the feelings of a bird when it is caught in the trap of the bird-catcher. It loses its freedom and is in the control of the bird-catcher. Not only is it prevented from flying freely, it can barely take a few steps. It is confined by man to a cage. Its suffering or pleasure, its peace or danger, is entirely in the hands of man. It may scream and weep and wail; it may fear or tremble. That is one way in which we are tested by God and that is one way He disciplines us.

A man may carry a heavy burden until he has difficulty in breathing, until his muscles are taut and his bones aching. He has no strength to move and he longs with all his heart for someone to come and help and relieve him for a little while. That is another way in which we are tested by God and that is another way He disciplines us.

Then we come to those who would ride their chariots over us and crush our heads. We cannot bear even to think of an experience like this. Our head is not made of brass or iron. Yet if God allows anyone to ride his chariot over us He is certainly able to protect us and to keep our heads from being crushed completely. In fact He can keep us from even being injured. Nevertheless, the pain and the shame in such an experience are unavoidable. Yet there are times when God allows us to be tested and disciplined even to this point.

The Psalmist spoke of the three kinds of suffering just described. But he could sum up the experience in the words: 'We went through fire and through water; but Thou broughtest us out into a wealthy place.'

Passing through fire and water is not only a painful

experience it is also a dangerous experience. But because it is the will of God the peril can be transmuted into peace, and danger into tranquillity. As a result we are brought out into a wealthy place. The testing and discipline are hard to endure, but when we know the outcome we can greet it joyfully. The Psalmist related his experiences in order to help others in the midst of testing and discipline. I too shall be happy if my testimony can bring comfort and encouragement to those who are being tried. Let me then relate something of the way that God brought me through fire and water into a wealthy place.

Spiritual Exercises

In the previous chapter I told of my return to teach at the school in Baoding in the autumn of 1920. A few days before I left Peking I was very troubled in my heart because both my mother and my sister were far from the Lord. For a long time I had wanted to help them but it had never come about. On the day before my departure I was in my own room weeping. Just at that moment my sister came in and seeing me weeping she also wept. I said to her, 'It is because my mother and my sister are far from the Lord that I am sad at heart.' I then exhorted her a little. My sister confessed her sin and told me earnestly that she was willing to repent. Taking my hand she wept for a very long time. This made me indescribably happy.

The next day (September 8th) I took an early train to Baoding. But after only a day or two my ear was so painful and swollen that I had to return to Peking. I stayed there for 16 days. During that time I talked further with my sister. Her response brought me comfort and joy. I eventually left Peking on October 4th to return to Baoding.

During the previous term I had made preparations to organize a branch of the YMCA and this term I prepared to hold a special inaugural meeting. From the outside it seemed that we made good progress, but my own heart was empty and extremely weak. I was pessimistic and conscious of lack of power. In addition to all this I was troubled by some short-sightedness in both my eyes and the condition seemed to be daily worsening. I feared that deterioration would continue and I couldn't imagine what the future held. I had worn glasses when I was 14; and the lenses had been changed when I was 18. After a year the condition became worse and the lenses were changed three times. It seemed that if the deterioration continued I should soon be little different from a man without sight.

Nevertheless it was my own spiritual poverty that gave me most pain at that time, and the fact that my work was powerless. When I saw the darkness and corruption in the church I became disappointed and melancholy. I was conscious of the importance of God's commission to me and of the heaviness of my responsibility.

On the evening of November 21st I was talking in the school with a newly-arrived colleague. He raised the question of sin. In my heart I became very angry. How could any sin remain in a good Christian like me? My colleague talked of sins like pride. He said, 'Some believers are very enthusiastic and they work indus-triously. But they do this not to glorify God but to glorify themselves.' These words pricked my heart for they described exactly the cause of my disease and its symptoms. My attitutude changed from anger as I came to agree with him and finally I was deeply moved.

I returned to my own room and knelt by my bed confessing my sins.

At that time I had been a believer more than six years and during that period I had made some spiritual progress. Every day without fail I would pray and read the Bible. I made myself attend services of worship. I contributed a tenth of my income for the work of the Lord. I watched my lips lest I gave utterance to unclean language. I was not avaricious. I never had any illicit relationship with one of the other sex. I was faithful in carrying out my official duties. I respected and loved my sister. I zealously served the students and had led some of them to join the church. Those who knew me — apart from those who envied me — mostly respected me and had confidence in me. After I had completed one year's teaching the Principal said to me, 'If you are not going to undertake further studies you must on no account accept an invitation elsewhere; we greatly need you and you must come back here.' All these things gave me a feeling of self-satisfaction and made me regard myself as 'the favourite of heaven.' I considered myself greatly superior to other believers and leaders and elders and pastors in the church. Apart from my awareness that there were many church leaders whose character was depraved I felt that there were not many of my calibre with ideals like me.

Self-examination

But that evening, when I knelt by my bed to confess my sins, everything was changed. Everybody else faded out and I was left alone with God. I became conscious of the depravity within me. I began to see that the sins committed by other people were parallelled in my own heart. The only difference was that the sins of others were manifest while my own sins were hidden. But I began to understand that when God looks on man He sees not as man sees, only the outside, but He sees what is inside. In the presence of God I feared and trembled. The more I prayed the more conscious I became of my unworthiness. I was unclean, vicious, and hateful. I uttered no sound as I knelt by my bed but I was humbled to the dust. My experience taught me one thing. No matter how good a man is, only let him be illumined by the Spirit of God and he becomes conscious of his own utter depravity. I realized that were it not for the blood of Christ I would have no hope whatever of entering the presence of God. I dedicated myself anew to Him. I was willing to obey Him fully. I was ready to serve Him faithfully all my life. From that day on my life was gradually but wonderfully changed.

In the days when I was a student in the Middle School I entered into the activities of the YMCA. Often I appealed for subscriptions to meet the expenses of the Association. This method of raising money was commonplace and I naturally regarded it as appropriate. And when in November 1920 we held the inaugural meeting for the local branch of the YMCA at the school in Baoding we raised a loan to buy a large quantity of food to entertain the guests as well as the teachers and students in the school. Afterwards I went with several officers in the Association to solicit funds so that we could repay the loan we had incurred. I was at that time suddenly shown by the Holy Spirit that to solicit subscriptions in this way was not fitting. I also realized that in establishing a local branch of the YMCA, although we truly hoped that it would help the students, part of my motive was to add to my own fame. I reproved myself for this, but since we could not break the group up, we found ourselves in a position from which there was no retiring: (as we say in China we were unable to get down from the tiger's back).

Baptism by immersion

At this time the question of baptism arose. One of my colleagues talked to me about his experience of baptism. What he said aroused my intense astonishment. From my earliest days I had regularly attended worship with my mother. Throughout all the years since then I had only known of baptism as a sprinkling of water on the head. I had never heard of anyone being baptized by immersion. When he told me that he had been baptized by immersion I asked him why He replied: 'The Lord Jesus and His disciples did it this way.' I returned to my room and applied myself diligently to searching the Scriptures. As a result of this I concluded that I myself ought to be baptized by immersion. Having come to this conclusion I talked it over with the students. In doing this I aroused opposition from the church authorities. On one occasion, at morning worship, one of the leaders argued against what I had advocated. This is what he said: 'Naturally we ought to believe the Bible. But when we read the Bible we must choose what is good and believe it, and what is not good we should not believe. It is like eating fish. We can only eat the flesh; we cannot swallow the bones and sharp pieces.' He also said: 'It is naturally important to believe doctrine. But we are living in the world and we should regard practical matters as more important than doctrine. In the world no one can be perfect.' Another leader when preaching made the following statement: 'When Jesus was baptized it was admittedly in the River

Jordan. But this does not mean that he was immersed in the water . . . A certain Roman Catholic Church has an ancient picture showing Jesus standing in the water and John using his hands to scoop up water to sprinkle on His head.' These leaders were hoping to make me abandon my desire to be baptized by immersion. In the event their inaccurate explanations only strengthened my resolve to go ahead.

The colleague who had talked to me and who had given me not a little guidance through his testimony was eventually expelled from the school. He left Baoding for Peking on December 20th. I escorted him to the station since I particularly respected his readiness to be persecuted for the Truth and his refusal to surrender. I said to him, as I grasped his hand in parting, 'I also am prepared to make sacrifices.' I asked him if he would introduce me to someone who would baptize me by immersion.

He introduced a teacher named Ju who came on December 29th from Peking to discuss the matter and I prepared to be baptized before long in the river. On January 2nd 1921, I informed Mr Wong, the responsible officer in the school, of my decision. He then warned me on no account to be deceived. For a moment I weakened, and doubts arose. I also feared that I would lose my position. So it was with a feeling of disappointment that I left his room. I then sought out the three students whom I regarded with respect and I talked and prayed with them. As a result my purpose was again strengthened. That evening at 10 o'clock the school Principal and Mr Wong came to see me together. They told me that if I were to be baptized by immersion then I would have to leave the school immediately. Those students who also wanted to be immersed would also have to leave. The Principal added that they were very reluctant to let me go and he urged me to think the matter over very seriously for a couple of days before coming to a final decision. Should I change my mind and decide against being baptized they would welcome my continuing at the school. But otherwise I would have to leave. We talked together until midnight.

Test of faith

So two possible paths lay before me. One path was to go ahead and to be baptized by immersion. But what would this involve? I faced at least three difficulties. First, I would immediately lose my occupation. Second, my reputation would suffer. Up to that time I had been very concerned about 'face', and I had enjoyed fame. If I were obliged to resign in the middle of term it would truly be a matter of shame. Third, my future plans would come to nothing. As mentioned earlier, Mr Thomas Biggin had expressed his hope to raise funds for me to engage in further studies in England. But if I went ahead and were immersed I would be regarded by the London Mission as a rebel and naturally they would be unable to subsidize my studies any longer. If I had to support myself as a student even one year would be beyond my reach, let alone the 10 years or even 8 years which I had had in view. I dare not think how dark and fearful the future would be if I went ahead with my desire to be baptized by immersion.

The other path was infinitely easier. All I needed to do was to set aside my intention to be immersed and the three difficulties would immediately evaporate. I could continue in the school as a teacher and in the future I could enter the university and be supported by the Mission.

The issue for me was whether I would be obedient to God or disobedient. Only recently had I confessed my sins to Him and promised Him that I would dedicate myself wholly and obey Him completely. Now I was faced with a command from God and it would be a test of my obedience. In the face of this dilemma I was like an ant on a hot saucepan, not knowing what to do for the best.

Suddenly a thought came to my mind. 'Since being immersed is the pattern in the Bible I must naturally act accordingly. However, it does not matter if I delay several years. After I return from England I can accept a responsible position in the church, and with position, authority, and prestige, I can then be immersed without fear of intervention. I can not only be immersed myself but I can direct other people to be immersed. Is not this a case of having a perfect answer to both questions?' With this thought my heart was temporarily at peace.

Obedience
However, not long afterwards another thought came to me: what God looks for is obedience to His commands. 'To obey is better than sacrifice, and to hearken than the fat of rams.' If I delay baptism in order to evade difficulties I am rebelling against God. How can one who rebels against God consider being a student in a Theological College? If I have a duty to perform and fail to do it in order to escape trouble, how can I hope to be used by God? The thought of delay again caused unrest, and I felt that I should go ahead and be baptized immediately. The two ideas struggled in my heart like two wrestlers. But I

concluded finally that my own gain or loss was not a factor; I must simply obey God. Even so the battle raged for several days.

On the afternoon of January 4th, as the sun was about to set, the Principal came to my room to enquire how I had made my decision. I explained what I intended to do. He then took a bag of coins to cover my fare to Peking asking me to leave the school that evening. I told him that I could not leave at that moment since the three daily trains from Baoding to Peking had already gone. And even if I were to stay in an inn I needed a little time to collect my belongings and to hand over my responsibilities. He finally gave me permission to stay overnight but asked me not to allow pupils to come to my room that evening. He feared that I would stir up the students and encourage them to seek baptism. I promised that I would not invite students to my room but that I would not hinder any who wanted to come and say goodbye.

Personal witnessing

When the students heard that evening that the Principal had expelled me they came to my room one after another. I preached to them and I exhorted them. I was conscious of being full of power. The few days of fear and anxiety had gone. I read with them the words of Scripture: 'Whosoever will save his life shall lose it: and whosoever will lose his life for my sake shall find it' (Matthew 16:25). I said to them: 'Students! What I have today given up for the Lord Jesus is but a small thing; my Lord will compensate me many times over.' When I uttered these words I had no idea how he would compensate me, but thanks be to His Name, they were prophetic and the prophecy was perfectly fulfilled. That evening I produced cakes which I had bought from the tea shop several days before, and I divided them up for the students to eat as a farewell memory. Not until one o'clock in the morning did we go to bed.

The next day, at morning worship, the Principal made an announcement. Since Teacher Wong Ming-dao proposed to be baptized by immersion he had been asked to leave the school. If any students also wished to be immersed they too would be asked to leave. Five students declared without hesitation that they would also be leaving the school. Four of these desired like me to be baptized by immersion. The other one had no thought of being baptized but since for more than a year he had travelled the heavenly road with me, to remain after my expulsion would be giving offence. So in order to comfort me and as a mark of sympathy, he too withdrew from the school. That particular student has had continuous fellowship with me for 29 years, and now, as ever, he is my fellow-servant. He is Mr Shih Tien-min (Tien-min means Heavenly People or Heavenly Citizen).

I do not in any way blame the Presbyterian Church school for expelling me. As representatives of their denomination they calculate that they can do no other than make me give up my position. Apart from the straightforward question of immersion there was another reason. Various preachers belonging to a certain group had on one occasion stirred up considerable disorder and division among the Presbyterian churches in that area, and on account of it the churches had suffered severe losses. Teacher Ju who wanted to baptize me belonged to that particular group and so the school was naturally very cautious. This was another reason why they could do no other than expel me.

Baptized

In the afternoon of the 5th we five took our baggage and left the school. We stayed overnight at an inn. There again arose thoughts of doubt and fear in my heart, and my mind was vacillating and restless; I suffered acutely. The next day we set out to find a place with water for the baptisms. It was the period of 'Little Cold' and a few days earlier it had snowed for two whole days. The ground everywhere was covered with a blanket of pure white snow, and the river was frozen over with thick ice. We went along the city moat, towards the south, looking for a

suitable place. We came to a bridge over the river and underneath the bridge was a sluice. The water from above the sluice cascaded down like a small waterfall. Because of the constant movement at this point the water could not solidify into ice and what we saw was like a small pool. There we stopped. After we had prayed, standing on the snow, Mr Ju went down into the water. The four students and I then took off our wadded garments and put on thin garments. We then went down into the water. Shih Tien-min, the student who had left school out of sympathy for me, decided on the spur of the moment to join us. He was also baptized. I still remember how, as I came up out of water, my long hair turned immediately into a stick of ice. As soon as I took off the thin garments they became hard and solid like thin boards.

Pentecostal teaching

We returned to the inn. Mr. Ju then directed us to seek the Holy Spirit. This is the teaching most emphasized by the Pentecostals. The Pentecostal groups in China previously included the Pentecostal Church, the Apostolic Faith Church, and the Church of God. Today they are mostly known as the Assemblies of God. They maintain that speaking in tongues is the one and only sign of receiving the Holy Spirit, so those who have never spoken in tongues are regarded as not having received the Holy Spirit. Mr Ju worked in a small Pentecostal Church in the city of Peking. Originally he was a coal merchant but because of zeal for the Lord he gave up his business to become a preacher. He is a devout and sincere believer, well acquainted with the Bible. But he did not greatly understand the truths of the Bible and he lacked general knowledge.

On the day after we were baptized, at 10 o'clock in the morning, Mr Ju came again to the inn to pray that we might receive the Holy Spirit. He preached to us the ten commandments in detail. That afternoon after 3 o'clock all five students spoke in 'tongues' leaving only me who had not spoken. The next day (the 8th) I prayed earnestly the whole day, but I still had not spoken in tongues. On the 9th, at 3 o'clock in the afternoon, we again prayed together in the inn. My tongue produced some incomprehensible sounds and Mr Ju announced that I was speaking in tongues, and that I had received the Holy Spirit. But in fact I was not conscious of any change at that time. It had been on November 21st, when I confessed my sins to the Lord, that I was conscious of a marked change. Rather than the day when I uttered sounds which could not be understood, it was the day when I confessed my sins, and obeyed God's commandments, giving up everything, that I was filled with the Holy Spirit.

Mr Ju had taught us simply to cry 'Hallelujah' and to repeat those syllables in succession without stopping. Thus it seemed to be the manufacture of tongues by a man. Naturally we did not regard Mr Ju, who was a sincere and devout man, as having deceived us. Rather he was deceived himself, and through his own lack of commonsense it was he himself who suffered loss.

Home again
I set out for home on the 10th. The weather was very gloomy. Frost clung to the branches of trees and to the telegraph wires; and it was very cold. As the engine's whistle sounded I took my leave of Baoding where I had lived for a year and a half.

While I was travelling home I felt that after the sacrifice that I had made for truth my mother and elder sister would compliment me and praise me. But it was not at all like that. As soon as my mother heard the details of my leaving school all she could do was to rebuke me thoroughly, blaming me for throwing everything away in order to be baptized. When my sister came home from school and heard of my experiences she also was greatly disappointed. And when the news got around I was widely misunderstood. Some said I was suffering from a mental disorder; others said that I had been deceived. My baptism did not interest them; they only felt that I ought not to have sacrificed my position and my future. Some said, 'There are people who, in order to get support for study, have accepted baptism. There are also people who in order to get a job in the church have professed to believe in the Lord. You already had a position in the church, and you had the prospect of help for future study. But now on account of your beliefs you have sacrificed them all.' I answered them: 'In ancient times many believers on account of their faith gave up their homes and gave up their lives; none of them drew back. If you compare what I have done with what they did my sacrifice is very small.' They said, 'Those people followed myths. People in the present generation should not believe myths like this.' As I listened to them I realized that although these people were Christians by name, they were not in fact believers at all. My eyes were opened and I began to distinguish between true Christians and false Christians.

Increasing trials

The fires of trial grew fiercer. Neither my mother nor my sister understood me. Those who knew me both ridiculed and reviled me. Those who were concerned about me sighed for me. My heart was on fire but my spiritual understanding was limited. Because of this I was biased in my conversation and behaviour. I acknowledge that the persecution which I received at that time was in part because of my beliefs and obedience to the Lord and in part because of my immature and biased attitudes.

Being surrounded by hostility was indeed an unpleasant experience. I felt that if only I could find a job I would lessen the grief at home and reduce misunderstandings among my acquaintances. But who was willing to introduce a person with a mental illness for a job? And who would engage someone with a mental illness? My mother pressed me to go out and to do something. Alternatively, I could go to Mr Thomas Biggin and confess my errors, acknowledging that it was a mistake to have been baptized by immersion and requesting help even yet to go to university. I should like to have taken the first of these two paths, but I could not. As for the second I could not acknowledge my baptism as an error for the simple reason that it was not an error. Yet my mother thought it was. It pained her and it pained me that we should have this difference over a matter of beliefs.

During that period I was reluctant to go outside the front gate of our courtyard, because as soon as I got outside I would meet people with whom I was acquainted and some whom I wished to avoid. Of course to live at home doing nothing was also very hard to take. There were only the three of us in the family and the other two did not understand me. There was also an aunt in the courtyard who understood me even less, and what she had to say about it only added to my mother's pain. One night in a dream I was driven outside the main gate by my mother who ordered me to leave home. I was crying in a loud voice and pleading with my mother to let me have my wadded gown and other garments. But she refused to give them to me. I began to weep. Then I awoke and found myself still weeping. In reality my compassionate mother could never act in this way. Yet the dream was an expression of my bitter sorrow at that time.

God's mercy

My heart rebelled against God. In order to obey His commands I had accepted this suffering, and yet God had not opened for me a way of escape. He had allowed my suffering to continue. He was unjust, unfaithful, and uncompassionate. No longer could I serve a God like this. I did not question God's existence, but how could I continue serving Him? Why should I not take the path of my own choosing? It was a moment of great danger for me. Had I, on that day, abandoned God I think I would have left the world within a year or two in great pain. But thank God, He did a wonderful thing. He manifested

His power and at that time of crisis for me He led me to read 1 Corinthians 10:13: 'There hath no temptation taken you but such as is common to man; but God is faithful who will not suffer you to be tempted above that ye are able; but will with the temptation also make a way to escape, that ye may be able to bear it.'

No passage of Scripture could have been a greater help or comfort. I had thought that my temptation was too heavy; I had thought that God was unfaithful. But here was the answer. He showed me also that He would make for me a way of escape. What had I to complain about?

I must tell here of another special experience. One morning my mother said to me, 'Ming-dao, last night I prayed for you and asked God to make you come to yourself. Then I suddenly heard a voice saying, ' Forty days and nights in the wilderness." I think that you are being deceived by the Devil. You must quickly come to yourself.' As soon as I heard this I realized that these words were spoken to bring home to me the fact that I was being tempted by the Devil. I remembered that it was through the word of God that the Lord Jesus overcame Satan and I must overcome him in the same way. So I applied myself particularly to the study of the Bible.

A deep grasp of God's word

In the courtyard we had a room which had originally been used as a shelter for plants and to which we had added a door and windows to make it habitable. It was there that I prayed; it was there that I studied my Bible; it was there that I sometimes fasted. Although I had been reading the Bible regularly for more than six years it was as if all the passages about the way of life had been covered with a sheet of paper. This was teaching I had never understood. But all of a sudden my heart was opened wide and I grasped the fact that Christ could give eternal life to all who believe in Him. In Him is life. And it is life He gives to all who trust Him. He Himself rose from the dead; and He makes those who believe in Him to rise from the dead as well. He Himself has overcome death, and this is the victory He gives to those who trust Him.

With a new understanding of the doctrine of life I realized that death was not to be feared. The pleasures of the world were not strong enough to hold us. The fame and empty glory that I had previously sought for became so insignificant that they were not worth even a glance. I now abandoned completely all thought of becoming someone important. No matter what God commanded, whether big or small, it was mine to obey.

I had read the Bible every day since I believed in the Lord at the age of fourteen. I also believed the Bible. I believed that Jesus died and rose again. But I had not really understood the resurrection. My thoughts about life after death were also vague. As I studied the Bible I clearly understood that the body of Jesus was assuredly raised after three days, that He left the tomb and that after forty days He ascended to heaven. More than this I learnt that according to His promise the Lord Jesus would come from heaven to receive His disciples; and that the saints who were sleeping would be raised from their graves to receive a body which was glorious and incorruptible. At the same time the saints still living would be changed and be given a glorious body that would never die, and that together with the saints who had been raised from the dead they would be taken up to be for ever with the Lord.

These truths are clearly recorded in the Bible. And the Bible had been in my hands a number of years. Yet I could not recall having read them. Certainly they had never made any impression. Someone with spiritual insight has used an illustration to describe this experience. 'Some of God's promises are written as it were with invisible ink. It is only when they are placed in the flame of suffering that they become manifest.' So it was with me. The intense suffering of that period was like a fire which made the promises of God become visible.

The empty glory and fame which I had previously desired and sought for, I could now only see as refuse. I now understood that in order to do the work of God it was not essential to go to a theological college. The important thing was to use time to read the Scriptures and to be trained and taught by God. So I now abandoned my plans to go successively to a university and a theological college in China and then later to go to England. I only asked God to give me time to read through the Bible several times. My prayer was answered, thank God! It was not long before He gave me a splendid opportunity to do this.

Opportunity for Bible Study

I have a cousin who at that time was a superintendent in military hospital attached to the 13th Division in the Army. His home was in a village outside the wall of the city Yi-ho-yuen. One day he came to visit my mother and he said to her: 'Aunt, I hear that my cousin is mentally unwell. This is very lamentable. However, it does not mean that there is no hope of a cure. It is important for him to be contented. So on no account reprove him or oppose him. You must follow his ideas and say what pleases him; in that way he will gradually become normal again.' He also proposed that I go to stay with him. 'Cousin!' he said, 'I know that in the ordinary way you like to travel in the mountains and amuse yourself in the water. It happens that my home is close to the Mountain of

Ten Thousand Lives where the mountains stand out clearly and the water is luxuriant. My wife and I would like you to come and stay with us and relax for a while. If you want to read the Bible, you can read it in my home.' As soon as I heard what he proposed I recognised that this was a path that God was opening for me. So I accepted his invitation. I duly left home to stay with them on March 16th.

My cousin and his wife both urged me not to despise the pleasures of the world. At the back of their minds was the hope that I would abandon my faith and turn my back on the Lord whom I served. But I for my part exhorted them to repent without delay and to believe in the Lord. But neither side could persuade the other, so we gradually gave up talking on these subjects.

The village of Da-ye was truly a lovely spot. The pines and cedars, the bridge over the river, the mountains and the streams of crystal clear water — all combined to create a scene of exquisite beauty. When I moved there it was just before the vernal equinox. It was the time of buds and blossom, and the warmth of spring was in the air. Every day I rose early and took my Bible to Crouching Tiger Mountain. Sitting on the stones at the riverside I would study my Bible and pray. I also found pleasure watching the tiny fish swimming in the stream. I watched the sun setting over the distant mountains. Sometimes I would go to a nearby cemetery and there again I would read my Bible and meditate. When the weather was fine I would climb to the top of the hill and there sing hymns and pray. From time to time I would meet a countryman and talk to him about the Gospel.

I had two methods of reading my Bible. One method was to read the whole book from beginning to end. Another way was to study important themes. The 62 days I spent in Da-yu were like attending a short-term Bible School. I read the Bible right through

six times. I certainly made considerable progress in my understanding of the Truth.

God's call recognized

On May 28th I received a letter from my old friend Teacher Chun of Tsang-Hsien. He had heard a report that I was mentally ill and he could only half believe it. He wanted me to explain my circumstances. Because I had great regard for his faith, his character, and his good sense, and also because I still had more than 10 dollars left, I felt that I should go and talk to him in Tsang-Hsien. So on June 27th I left Peking to travel via Tientsin to Tsang-Hsien. The next day I had a long talk with him. He then assured me that I was certainly not ill mentally and that I had been greatly blessed by God. He then invited me to preach in Tsang-Hsien. That was the first time that I preached in a church building after my call from God. I went back to Peking greatly comforted and encouraged. I was comforted because a respected friend had seen what the grace of God had done for me. I was encouraged because when I preached at Tsang-Hsien I was deeply conscious of the presence of God and enabled to speak with His power and authority.

On September 19th I received a letter from Mr Chun who said that the people in the church there had been very much moved and that both Western and Chinese workers there would like me to go again and to undertake several days' ministry. I was happy to do this and I actually spent more than three months in the area. As a result of this I was the more convinced that God had both chosen me for service and also given me the gifts and power to carry it out. I felt that God would soon open up wider ministry. But contrary to expectations I found myself confined to petty jobs around the house.

Learning patience

Why did God choose me and then not use me? I couldn't understand it. And why did I have to suffer so much? It was a mystery. I was already 22 years old and yet I was still unable to support my mother. Indeed, it was my mother's food that I was eating. How could I make her burden lighter? I could not find the answer. When I was a Middle School student I depended on getting a scholarship to attend university. When I was doing the one-year Preparatory Course I was supported by the London Mission. As a teacher I could depend on my salary to support myself. My sister's livelihood was catered for by her teaching. My mother was able to live on the rent from the rooms in our courtyard and she even took from this to help me. Naturally my mother and sister were prepared to share their food with me, but I could not bear to be beholden to them indefinitely. I tried to make their burdens lighter. Every morning I swept the rooms and the courtyard; I went out to buy food; I returned and lit a fire to cook it. After the meal I would wash the dishes, do the laundry, and mend the bedding. My mother could not bear to see me engaged in chores like this and she urged me to go out and find a job so that we could hire a young girl to help around the house.

Sometimes I would weaken and spend time looking for a job, and sometimes people would bring openings to my notice. But I was really waiting to do the work of a preacher. Yet my perplexity was mounting. I blamed God and I said to Him: 'Previously when it was my ambition to be a politician you called me to preach the Truth. I am now willing to be a preacher in accordance with your call but you make me spend my days engaged in arduous and inferior chores like this. Why do you treat me so harshly?' I felt so bitter about it at times that I did not want to live. Sometimes when engaged in manual work I became so frustrated that I threw things on the ground. But one day when I was reading the Book of Exodus I saw how God took Moses into the desert of Midian to look after the sheep and how he stayed there for forty years. I understood from that how we can learn many lessons while engaged in lowly chores. This helped me to work diligently and faithfully in the home and to carry out my tasks as beautifully and satisfactorily as I could. God taught me that doing jobs around the home was as important as preaching. I also realized that if I did these immediate jobs badly I would later on do my work of preaching badly. And even if God kept me doing lowly chores for a whole life-time I would say to Him 'Amen!' Originally I had wanted to be a great politician. Later I had wanted to be a great evangelist. But only when God had cured me of this longing for 'greatness' did He begin to commit His work to me.

Further preaching

During 1922, apart from doing the chores of the home, I daily set aside time in my little hut for searching the Scriptures. I spent the first part of 1923 in the same way. On July 31st, 1923, I took the train on the Peking-Hankow Line to Yuen-Shi Hsien. After alighting I made my way to the home of a former pupil. Then at the China Inland Mission in Zan-Hwong Hsien I spoke at an eight days' convention. I planned to visit my friend Shih Tien-min but en route I became ill. I returned to Peking and the illness took a turn for the worse. Thus I remained at home until the

end of the year, partly working and partly searching the Bible.

In March 1924 I was invited together with more than thirty preachers, Chinese and Western, from all churches in the city, to go and take part in an evangelistic campaign at an army camp farther south. It was the first time that I had joined workers from all the churches. Unhappily the things I saw and heard caused me great anxiety (lit. headache and heartache). A few amongst these preachers made a good impression, but for the most part they were truly unworthy to be called the servants of God. As a result of the six days' evangelism there were more than 3,000 baptized. But it was apparent by careful observation that only a few of them really repented and trusted the Lord. On the day when they all met enthusiastically for the baptismal ceremony I could not bear to be a spectator, and I returned by train to the city. This experience only made me recognize all the more clearly the corruption, the emptiness and the poverty of the churches in China. It stirred me to give myself all the more enthusiastically to the work of the Lord.

As we moved into summer I travelled a good deal engaged in special meetings. I also stayed for 12 days in Jinan with a brother who had corresponded with me for some time and we were a great encouragement to each other. On August 30th I went to De-Hsien to speak at meetings for leaders in the Congregational Church and churches of the London Mission. I heard that an unconverted evangelist was distorting Bible truth in his preaching and ruining the faith of the congregation. I was greatly disturbed about this and taking my courage in both hands I took the opportunity, in the middle of the meetings, to point out his errors one by one. Predictably I aroused the ire of all the members of his particular group and they wildly cursed and attacked me. This was the first occasion on which I had publicly declared war on evil forces within the church. Thank God, He led me in triumph in Christ.

The Peking work begins

Returning from this itinerary I stayed as before in my home, partly working and partly studying the Bible. Just at that time a neighbour who lived in the outer courtyard moved away and a room (of two sections) became vacant. By this time I had a certain amount of income of my own, and after I had talked with my mother she allowed me to have the use of the room and I was able to make a contribution towards the expenses of the home. The hut which I had been making use of was too small for me, for people were now coming frequently to examine the

Scriptures with me. The number of these callers could now be increased, and on October 18th we began to hold meetings in my new accommodation. There was an attendance of three. The next week it was increased to five. We then met every Saturday, sometimes with few, sometimes with more. From December 24th we added a Wednesday Bible Study Meeting. Thus it was that my work of preaching began in Peking.

During 1924 I wrote several small booklets which were printed and distributed. Four were published that year entitled (i) A most important matter, (ii) Trumpet call in an evil world, (iii) The Christian and Idols, (iv) The Christian's Cross. Each had 64 pages. This was the beginning of my literary work.

Change of views

In the spring of 1925 the work opened up tremendously. I will describe this in the next chapter. What I want to do here is to go back a few years and to relate something of the modification in my beliefs between 1921 and 1924. After my expulsion from the school at Baoding and my return to Peking, I attended the meeting connected with the Mr Ju who had baptized me. Previously known as the Hsin-Hsin Hwei (Faith and Heart Church) it had now changed its name to 'The Church of God'. The leader there was an elderly Norwegian. When well attended the meeting numbered over twenty people. They had no chapel but met in the guest room of a private house. Like other Pentecostal evangelists this elderly person insisted that if a person did not speak in tongues it meant that he or she had not received the Holy Spirit. He also advocated that we keep the seventh day as our Sabbath. But he accepted what was put forward by a believer from New Zealand that the first day in Asia was really the seventh day. Because of this believers in Asian countries should regard Sunday as the seventh-day Sabbath whereas in the countries of Europe and America the Sabbath was on Saturday. He did not believe that those who repented and believed could be saved. He insisted that nothing in the world could be as easy as that. He declared that after a person had believed in the Lord he should pursue holiness until he had got rid of all sin. Only then could he be saved. The method he taught of getting rid of sin was even more ludicrous. He made a list of all the sins recorded in the New Testament, 83 in all, and this he hung up in the room. He made people read through the list every day. By doing this, he said, people would gradually get rid of the sins and become holy. He also taught other strange doctrines. Those who followed him were mostly lacking in commonsense; some were illiterate and some could only read the Bible. When I first attended the meetings there I was somewhat inclined towards this group, but as time went on I became more and more dissatisfied.

Although I was not satisfied with what this elderly person preached, there was one point in which I was still in agreement with him. It was that 'Unless you are holy you cannot be saved.' From the time when I first believed in the Lord I fiercely hated sin and longed for holiness. When I committed sin I was greatly distressed and greatly chided myself. When I saw other people sin I was very pained. All kinds of sin were apparent in the church, and I was filled with righteous anger. I could not believe that so-called believers who were in the habit of sinning could be saved. I knew that God hated sin even more than I did. So I decided that those who did not forsake their sin and become holy could not be saved. With this kind of belief, my heart was continually in a state of unrest. I had not yet completely forsaken my sin, I was still not sufficiently holy, so I dare not say that I was saved. I believed that the Lord Jesus could give men eternal life, but when it came to the point, could I be saved? I had no guarantee. At that time if a believer had said in my hearing that he was saved I would certainly have reproved him for being presumptuous. With no assurance of salvation I was constantly in a state of conflict and apprehension, lest after a lifetime of believing the Lord I should end up by being rejected by Him. At the time I did not understand the doctrine of justification by faith, and all I did was to tremble with fear beneath Mount Sinai.

From law to grace

Now in the home of that elderly Norwegian there also lived an elderly Swede named Eric Pilquist. What he preached was quite different from what the elderly Norwegian preached. He constantly proclaimed the doctrine of justification by faith. He lived in a tiny room and wore extremely untidy clothes; he ate very plain Chinese food. He was very poor and was often ill. Seeing that he was old and had no means of support, I often went to visit him to give him a little comfort. He talked to me of being saved through faith. At first I could not receive his teaching but the passages of Scripture which he quoted at last began to work in my heart. By the spring of 1923 my thinking had begun to change.

When I was fully enlightened by the doctrine of justification by faith there was a great change in my beliefs. It was well that God had not earlier opened a door of ministry, for in that case I should have preached a distorted version of the truth. And how could I have rectified the results of that? From the time of my illumination I ceased to associate with the elderly gentleman who taught the law, and I associated more with the elderly gentleman who helped me to understand the doctrine of justification by faith. He handed to me some booklets in English explaining these doctrines, and he encouraged me to translate them into Chinese. Moreover the believers who received these small booklets made gifts which enabled me to carry on until the end of April, 1925, when I gave this work up. It also happened that in November that year Mr Pilquist became ill and passed away.

The Sabbath

From 1921 for several years I advocated keeping the Sabbath. I then discovered that the apostles nowhere in their letters taught the churches of the Gentiles to keep the Sabbath. Then doubts arose. After making it a matter of prayer and searching the Scriptures over a very long period I realized that God had never instructed the Gentiles to keep the Sabbath and that the practice of calling Sunday the Christian's Sabbath was simply tradition.

Speaking in tongues

In the matter of tongues I not only received the Pentecostal teaching at the time of my baptism but I also proclaimed it for more than a year. What I preached was this: 'When a believer receives the Holy Spirit he must speak in tongues, because speaking in tongues is the sole evidence of receiving the Holy Spirit; it means that all believers who have not spoken in tongues have not yet received the Holy Spirit.' Some testify that when they spoke in tongues they also acquired very great strength and that they spoke in tongues because they could not contain themselves, just as if there was a power controlling the tongue. With me it has never been like that. I uttered sounds which I did not understand by reason of endlessly repeating the word 'Hallelujah' as described earlier. At first I had no doubts. But doubts arose because some people simply repeated one sound such as 'Ba-ba-ba-ba' or 'Da-da-da-da' or 'Go-di, go-di, go-di!' for several minutes or even several tens of minutes, always repeating the same sounds. I ask, how can you call this 'tongues'? Even when angels speak they cannot use just one or two sounds to express many meanings . . . Another problem is that the manner of life of many who speak in tongues is particularly bad. During the two years 1921-1922 I knew a young man who had an intensely fierce nature. He ill-treated his wife so cruelly that it was enough to make a man's hair stand on end. He also had many other evil ways and could by no means be called a Christian. But as soon as he sat down he was able to speak in tongues. What he uttered was, moreover, not just a succession of similar sounds but something which sounded like a language. Looking at the question from another point of view I have also seen many sincere believers, devout in their manner of life, and zealously serving the Lord, full of the fragrance of Christ, and others who work for the Lord with power and authority, who have never spoken in tongues. Can it be that they do not possess the Holy Spirit? All these considerations caused me to give up the kind of teaching which I had received on being baptized.

God's word alone

The years that I spent at home devoting myself to the study of the Bible determined my subsequent attitudes. It was through this that I had to reject some of the teaching in the church which I had received when I was young. What I found in the Bible I received. What I did not find in the Bible I rejected. The truths of the Bible I believed; doctrines not in the Bible I was not prepared to believe. I had not read Bible commentaries. That kind of literature did not appeal to me. In my preaching and my teaching today the Bible is my only standard. Church traditions and man-made regulations were not my authority. Even less would I compromise with anything contrary to the truth. To me that was sinful. On no account would I give way to those who oppose God. Because of this I had to leave the church to which I originally belonged. I also had to sever relations with the church referred to above. I still did not know how God would use me. Still less had I any thought of starting a new work. So it was contrary to all expectation that God led me step by step to the position I hold today. I can only stand amazed when I contemplate the wonderful works of God.

To look back over the experiences of more than 20 years is not a difficult matter. During that period, however, I had to taste the flavour of unlimited misfortunes and to eat all kinds of bitterness. Sometimes a day was like a year; sometimes I suffered so acutely I wished to take my own life. Derision, misunderstanding, scoffing, persecution, grief — I have tasted them again and again. Who would anticipate that all of them would become the gains of today? 'We went through fire and through water; but Thou broughtest us into a wealthy place!' (Psalm 10-12). Previously I had only read the words of this Psalm. But now I have experienced them.

4.
A fortified city, an iron pillar and a bronze wall...

"Thou therefore gird up thy loins, and arise, and speak unto them all that I command thee: be not dismayed at their faces, lest I confound thee before them. For, behold, I have made thee this day a defenced city, and an iron pillar, and brazen walls against the whole land, against the kings of Judah, against the princes thereof, against the priests thereof, and against the people of the land. And they shall fight against thee; but they shall not prevail against thee; for I am with thee, saith the Lord, to deliver thee." (Jeremiah 1: 17-19)
The Lord said unto me, "Say not, I am a child: for thou shalt go to all that I shall send thee, and whatsover I command thee thou shalt speak. Do not be afraid of their faces: for I am with thee to deliver thee, saith the Lord.' (Jeremiah 1:7,8)

A fortified city, an iron pillar, and a bronze wall – these things are all hard and solid. They cannot easily be destroyed by the strength of men. If a man knocks against any of these things it is only he who suffers injury; on none of these things will he be able to inflict damage. God raised up Jeremiah to be a prophet, commanding him to speak for Him and to reprove the sins of the Jews. From the point of view of the obstinate, Jeremiah was clearly the enemy; he was in opposition to them. From the human point of view it was no different from taking an egg to strike a stone — courting one's own destruction. Yet because it was God who sent him, they could not overcome him. He was a fortified city, an iron pillar, and a bronze wall.

'Thou shalt go to all that I shall send thee, and whatsoever I command thee thou shalt speak.' Listening to these words which God spoke to Jeremiah we may say that Jeremiah was God's representative, God's messenger, and God's mouthpiece. God Himself did not go among the people, He sent Jeremiah as His representative and as His messenger. God Himself did not utter sounds and speak to the people; He raised up Jeremiah to be His mouthpiece. So naturally God would protect him and rescue him. And although on several occasions he was in peril, he was never poisoned by men's malice. To be a prophet of God is a mark of special favour, yet it is also a matter of hardship and danger. At the same time it is a position of security and stability.

I thank God that the commission He gave to Jeremiah is also the commission He gave to me. When I was in my twenties He commanded me to go and say the words that He wanted me to say. He saw that the darkness and corruption of the church was not greatly different from the darkness and corruption of the world. So He sent me on the one hand to be a trumpet call to the world and on the other hand to be a trumpet call to the church. He sent me to expose the darkness, corruption, depravity and unrighteousness both of the world and of the church. He sent me to summon men without delay to repent. Before I set out to speak on His behalf I was conscious of fear and trepidation. I realized that were I to reprove sin without allowing people to make excuses for sin I should inevitably provoke opposition and bring attacks upon myself. That is in fact what happened. On many occasions I was apprehensive and timid; I was tempted to remain silent; but in the event I could not restrain myself. My experiences of adversity were the same as Jeremiah's. This is what Jeremiah wrote: 'For since I spake, I cried out, I cried violence and spoil; because the word of the Lord was made a reproach unto me, and a derision daily. Then I said, 'I will not make mention of him, nor speak any more in his name.' But his word was in mine heart as a burning fire, shut up in my bones, and I was weary with forbearing, and I could not stay.' (Jeremiah 20:8,9).

If I spoke out, I encountered derision and opposition; if I did not speak out, then I could not contain myself. What did I do? I had to speak. Thank God, the more I spoke the greater the courage He gave me; the bolder I was, the greater my power. He made me become 'a fortified city, an iron pillar, a bronze wall.' I was encouraged by the words God spoke to Jeremiah: 'Be not afraid of their faces: for I am with thee to deliver thee' (1:8) and again 'They shall fight against theee; but they shall not prevail against thee; for I am with thee, saith the Lord, to deliver thee' (1:19). Strengthened by these promises

I was given the courage to rebuke sins in the world and apostasies in the church.

Irrespective of whether those concerned were wealthy and powerful, or whether they had prestige and position in the church, I proceeded without fear or favour to rebuke them. I urged them to repent, to abandon their wicked ways, and to return to God.

Exposing corruption

Not only do we find evil and apostasy in the church but we also find unethical practice. Christian leaders are engaged in 'cover-up'. In the secular world there has for many years been a practice known as 'Officials protect each other'. This is now common amongst leaders in the church. If it is an unbeliever who points to evil practices in the church the preachers will then say that he is resisting the truth and is the enemy of God. If it is a believer who points to evil practices in the church the preachers will then say that he is proud and arrogant, that he is criticizing the brothers, and that he is losing his love. The fact that evil exists within the boundary of the church is still not the most grievous aspect of the situation. The most grievous circumstance is that the leaders in the church refuse to repent and confess these sins – whether their own sins or those of the church – but they cleverly disguise them and cover them up. If in such a situation a person speaks out boldly and straightforwardly, and if he draws attention to the corruption and evil practices of both believers and preachers – in other words if he speaks out concerning those things that certain church leaders are unwilling to say, or unable to say, or which they do not dare to say – can it do any other than arouse their hatred and opposition?

Humanly speaking, if a person reprimands evils within the church without allowing a margin for excuses he will be opposed and rejected. Nevertheless if God wants to use a man He will open a door for him that no one can shut. Moreover, although the church in general has been corrupted, there are many believers in the churches who honour God and who mourn and grieve over sins in the church. For these reasons, although the message I preach arouses the anger of obdurate preachers and nominal Christians, yet the door of opportunity for ministry is everywhere wide open. During a period of twenty-four years God has taken me to 28 provinces of our country (and remember, a province is roughly the same size as England) and I have preached in churches connected with more than thirty denominations.

A positive response

Whenever I am invited to preach in a particular

church, I only agree to go that once. There is a reason for this. Irrespective of what the congregation are desirous of hearing I must sound the warnings and preach the messages that God lays on my heart. In the event I arouse their anger they will certainly not wish to invite me a second time. Naturally I do not intentionally arouse their anger, for God is by no means pleased if we go out and do battle for the sake of doing battle. The reason I rebuke sin and apostasy, without accepting any excuse, is that when I am confronted with these things I am filled with great anxiety (headache and heartache) and I simply cannot endure it. Another reason is that I have a deep sense of God's commission to do this. And woe is me if I fail to preach as He directs. I prefer to be attacked by men than to call forth the wrath of God. It is strange, when you think of it, that although I visit many places with the idea of paying one visit only, I am usually invited to go a second time and not infrequently for a third, fourth, and fifth time. This is evidence that within the churches there are still not a few worshippers of God who are ready to face His challenge.

A negative response

Naturally there are some churches which, after hearing me only once, regard me as if I am the plague and become very antagonistic. Their criticism of me is confined to statements such as: 'Proud and arrogant; considering himself right and others wrong', or 'Delighting in being critical and in exposing other people's shortcomings'. The commonest objection is: 'As soon as Wong Ming-dao starts presching he reviles people'. Actually the 'reviling' they speak of refers to the fact that I rebuke sin and unrighteousness. If we open the Bible we find that the ancient prophets all rebuked people in this way. Moreover their reproofs were far more serious than mine. Even our Lord, when He was on earth, rebuked people for their sins in uncompromising terms like this. If you read Matthew Chapter 23 you will see that what I say is true.

Some of God's servants are in themselves very pious and devout. They are aware of evil practices both in the world and in the church and they are extremely concerned about them. But they dare not speak out in plain words about these evils. Even less do they dare to reprove those who are responsible for the evils. The reason is, they fear to offend people; they fear to come into conflict with evil men. And because they fear to offend people they then fail to win people. We must reprove people, and allow no margin for excuses, but we must reprove people with a heart of love. Those who are unwilling to accept our reproof will become hostile and hate us, regarding us as enemies. But those who accept our rebuke and repent in sorrow before God will unreservedly thank us and love us; they will become our close friends. I thank God that as a result of more than twenty years work in Peking and the provinces I have made many close friends. I have also made not a few enemies who have gnashed their teeth at me. They do not hesitate to criticize me, to blaspheme me, and to attack me in the vilest language.

But those who love me never hesitate to do all they can to help me. During my illnesses they have treated me with the utmost kindness. I remember one occasion when I became very ill with diarrhoea in Jinan. Someone gave me two bottles of Lao Shan Mineral Water. I drank it during my illness and it did me good.

One brother heard about this and he quickly went to buy some more. But he had to go to quite a number of shops before he found it. He then bought six bottles, which was all they had. Maybe mineral water is a commodity which is not all that hard to get hold of. But the genuine love and zeal of that brother are qualities that money cannot buy.

An indictment of the Churches

Those who are unbelievers in the world of today need to listen to God's warning and call; the church of today has a similar need. Part of the commission that God has given me is to preach the Gospel to those who are outside the church so that they repent and believe. It is also part of my commission to call upon people in the churches to repent and forsake their sins. The condition of many churches today is truly deplorable. The buildings they have erected are pretentious and elegant. Inside you will find splendid furniture and fittings and also comfortable seats. Music and singing and a sermon made up of beautiful phrases all have their place. But in many places they are, in the eyes of God, like the empty shell of an egg. Only the eyes of God and the eyes of those who know the mind of God can discern the emptiness of many churches today. Such a church has only the outward trappings but the holiness, justice, sincerity, compassion, faith, and hope required by God have long ago declared bankruptcy.

Leaders in the churches serve for vain-glory; workers in the churches preach for wages; many of the members join the church for ulterior motives, or perhaps because they blindly follow others. Evangelists, in order to attract more church members and thus to increase the number on the church roll and also to swell the offerings, do not hesitate to accept large numbers indiscriminately. They do not enquire of the candidates what their faith is, what their life is, and what their character is. In this way the church becomes peopled with spurious believers. The church becomes noted for deception, lying, pretence, covetousness, bribery, subversion, hatred, envy, party spirit, division, licentiousness, uncleanness, and other hateful qualities. In fact the sins which flourish in the world are reproduced in the church. And two other heinous sins are added. One is that of presumptuous sin, and the other is that of hypocrisy. When unbelievers see the existence of sins like this in the church not only are they hindered from believing in the Lord they even blaspheme the Lord's name. Because of all this corruption and darkness in the church the weaker believers lose their faith; they stumble and fall. When the Lord Jesus saw the trade in oxen, sheep, doves, and the business of the money-changers in the precincts of the temple, He was filled with righteous anger. He took a whip to drive out the animals and He overturned the tables of the money-changers. Suppose He came again and visited the churches in the world today, how greatly, I wonder, would His anger today exceed His anger in the temple?

And what of the preachers? We cannot say, of course, that there are no good preachers. But we have to recognize that many of them simply regard preaching as a means of earning their living. Their eyes are on what they can get out of it and neither Creed nor Truth has a place in their reckoning. In order to acquire wealth they do not hesitate to lie, they do not hesitate to deceive, they do not hesitate to indulge in malpractices, they do not hesitate to derive personal gain from public funds. In order to acquire wealth they quarrel and brawl with their colleagues, they have confrontations with relatives and friends even in a court of law. Not only have they no regard for God, or beliefs, or conscience, they have no regard even for their own reputation or 'face'. They toady to people of position or affluence. To see their attitude when the wealthy or influential come to church makes us blush with shame.

Recently in this country there have been cases of officials who have been avaricious and corrupt to the highest degree and they possess both money and power. Because they have been baptized they have been regarded by some in the church as rare gems. The church has invited them to serve as members of the Board and also to preach. The church has also sought contributions from them. How can this disregard for high moral principles do other than bring great dishonour to God?

Christian preachers are often described by unbelievers as 'Foreign Priests' ('Priest' here meaning a Buddhist priest). I acknowledge that this is an expression, insulting preachers. Nevertheless if we pause for a moment and take a careful look at the manner of life and the activities of many preachers we would realize that this mode of expression is not entirely without reason. For there are not a few preachers who have never been called by God and who have never been commissioned by God. They are not in a position to call upon sinners to forsake their sins in order to escape the wrath of God. They cannot declare the Gospel to others; they cannot distribute to them the things which are needed by the spirit; they cannot deliver people from darkness and suffering. They cannot bring release to the captive;

they cannot bring comfort to the broken-hearted; they cannot show people the road they ought to travel; they cannot be a shepherd to the flock. They only deal with church affairs superficially. They lead a few meetings; they preach a little doctrine (albeit without enthusiasm); and when the time comes they receive a salary from the church to support their families. Are these practices basically different from those of a Buddhist priest in a Buddhist temple who constantly taps a wooden fish to beat time while he is chanting?

If preachers cannot make a real contribution to mankind and to the church, and if they merely depend on preaching as a means of livelihood, they cannot be called the servants of God. It would be more appropriate to call them the parasites of society. To be called by unbelievers a 'foreign priest' is a small matter; but to be rebuked by God is a most serious matter indeed.

In the churches sponsored by Westerners there is another deplorable phenomenon. Since the Western missionaries wield economic authority many people strive to accord with the missionaries' bent of mind and thus to gain some benefit. Chinese preachers who please the Western missionaries need have no anxiety about keeping their jobs. On the other hand a Chinese preacher who speaks plainly and without hypocrisy, and who has no thought whatever of ingratiating himself with those who hold the purse strings, may have more difficulty in winning employment under the Westerner. The danger is that those who have such high moral principles that they refuse to compromise may either feel themselves squeezed out or be compelled to withdraw by their own principles.

The preachers who remain in employment are then the double-faced small men. They are prepared to distort or sacrifice their own views in order to flatter and please the Westerner. They are just like the covetous officials of society. Yet the Westerners unanimously retain confidence in them and place great responsibilities on them. In my country most of the churches managed by Westerners are like this.

(Many Chinese, in conformity with the Chinese maxim 'not to break another man's rice-bowl' refrain from pointing out the misdeeds of a preacher employed by missionaries. It is plain that Mr Wong follows a higher principle).

With a depraved leadership what hope can there be that ordinary believers will develop? Unhappily the conditions described are not limited to just a few places, or to a few denominations. Churches throughout the whole country are like this. I grew up in a church environment. I studied at a Mission school for 10 years and became acquainted with not a few church members and preachers in the city of Peking. I now know even more of conditions in Peking. Ever since I began my itinerant ministry over 20 years ago I have become quite conversant with conditions in churches all over the country. Were I to relate what I have seen and heard of the deplorable circumstances in the churches I could fill a small book. There are, of course, many reasons for this widespread corruption. Chief among them is the fact that many have been received into the church who are not true Christians.

Why is it that many doctrines now current in the churches are unbiblical and in many cases contrary to the Faith? The answer is that many preachers are unbelieving preachers. The less intellectual among them preach doctrines that they themselves do not believe. The more intellectual among them take truths or facts from the Bible and they deal with them in a manner of speech described as 'like the reality but actually not so'; they thus distort the sense of a passage and preach it with a twisted interpretation. This is what they say: 'God is simply the great intelligence, the great power in the universe; He is the true, the good, the beautiful in the world. Jesus is simply the highest and the most ideal personality in the world. The death of Jesus was the highest manifestation of "sacrificing one's life to preserve one's integrity" or of "giving up life to obtain righteousness". They explain the resurrection of Jesus as being a case of "his spirit did not die" and "his influence remains". They say that the return of Jesus to take power is a symbolic way of saying that mankind all over the world believe in Jesus. The coming of the Kingdom is that we on earth use the teaching of Christ to set up an ideal society . . .' The cleverest of these preachers take the Bible truths believed by true believers and memorize them; they also have their own ways of interpreting them (as we see it) erroneously. When they meet true believers they preach the former; when they meet false believers or unbelievers they preach the latter . . .

A necessary ministry

So it came about that in my ministry, on the one hand, I had to attack sin, and on the other hand, I had to attack apostate teachings. When I attacked the former I called forth the reaction of the Pharisee-style 'False Morality Party'. When I attacked the latter I called forth the opposition of the Sadducee-style 'Party of Unbelief'. The former party said that I

reviled people; the latter party said that I was super-
stitious. I thus became a target. I do not blame them
for standing in opposition to me for I in fact first
stood in opposition to them. I was like Jeremiah who
was told that he was to stand against the whole land
— 'against the kings of Judah, against the princes
thereof, against the priests thereof, and against the
people of the land'. But in spite of opposition I did
not fear or withdraw, for the words addressed to
Jeremiah comforted me and strengthened me: 'They
shall fight against thee; but they shall not prevail
against thee, for I am with thee, saith the Lord, to
deliver thee."

Small beginnings

During the period 1921 to 1924 (already referred
to in various connections) I was on the one hand
mostly at home doing various arduous jobs around
the home; on the other hand I read the Bible and
waited to see how God would use me. Although I
travelled on a number of occasions for ministry in
various churches they were all for quite brief engagements and after the ministry I returned home to
engage in Bible study as before. It did not occur to
me then that the time was coming when I would be
invited to visit churches in every province. Nor did it
ever cross my mind that I should one day build a
meeting hall. Even less did I plan to engage in a settled
ministry. I simply recognized that I should diligently
and faithfully perform the duties that lay immediately
ahead of me. I thought no further than this.

At that time I understood one truth. 'He that is
faithful in that which is least is faithful also in much;
and he that is unjust in the least is unjust also in
much.' (Luke 16:10) So no matter what lowly jobs I

was doing, I always strove, in accordance with this teaching, to do them thoroughly (lit. most beautifully and most virtuously). When I was sweeping I allowed not even the slightest dust to remain in the room. When I cooked the meals I made a point of making them perfectly palatable and not allowing any of the food to lose its flavour. When I washed the clothes I made them perfectly clean. When I wrote a letter I wrote it very neatly, and even when it came to sticking on the stamp I stuck it on properly. In those days I had no hope of doing anything important (I had had such a hope between the ages of 14 and 20, but during the period from 21 to 24 that ambition had been removed by God). Nor did I know what kind of work God would entrust to me in the future. Yet the time was approaching when work in Peking would develop so tremendously that I could hardly cope. And it was not long before a widening ministry opened up for me outside Peking. I will relate how it happened.

The ministry develops

Throughout January and during the first part of February, 1925, two meetings were held in my home every week, one on Wednesday and one on Saturday. Those attending sometimes numbered as many as 14; sometimes there were as few as two. Then I was invited by a sister to speak on February 10th at a united women's meeting for all the churches in the city. It was a monthly meeting, and the meetings were held at each church in turn. On that occasion it was held at the West Drum Tower Presbyterian Church. Several tens of people were in attendance. I spoke that day on John 15: 1-8, the parable of the vine. After the meeting an elderly lady with a happy noble countenance came to the front and talked with me, asking for my name and address. She also enquired in which church I normally preached. I explained to her that I normally preached in my own home. She said to me that she had been considerably moved by the message and that she recognized that I had been chosen by God. Hearing that I was the son of Mr Wong Dzu-hou she told me that she had once known him but that after the Boxer Rising she had had no further news of the family. She added that meeting me had made her particularly happy. This elderly lady was Mrs Pan Wei-jou.

Most of the church leaders in Peking at that time regarded me as mentally unbalanced. For Mrs Pan to recognize me as one especially chosen by God was a circumstance that brought me immeasurable comfort and encouragement. From that time on she frequently introduced me to believers whom she knew, and since she was respected by all the churches in the city, her recommendations were naturally very effective, weighty, powerful, and influential. After that the attendance at the meetings in my home gradually grew. In the latter part of February we reached 13 or 14. At the beginning of March we moved up to more than 20. The room was too small. Then Mrs Pan invited me to speak at a meeting in her home every Friday. Then at the beginning of April a Mrs Yu who attended the meetings in my home made the suggestion that we meet in her home, which was quite commodious, on Sunday afternoons. I accepted the invitation and at the first meeting on April 5th more than 70 people attended. The meetings in her home were held altogether four times and each time we were overcrowded.

I was getting more invitations from churches in Peking and soon, on the average, I had a meeting almost every day. All these meetings meant constantly hurrying here and there all over the city and I began to feel weary. Then several believers got together and bought me a bicycle. This was a tremendous help and it enabled me to save both time and strength. On May 27th I left Peking to go to Nanking.

At this point I must tell a little of my motive in going to Nanking. During the years 1921 and 1922 I was particularly zealous. At the same time I regarded myself very highly. It was as if among all the Christians in the country there was not one more zealous than me — not one who loved the Lord more than me, or who understood the Truth more than me. Then in 1923 I began to subscribe to the Spiritual Light Newspaper (Ling-Gwong-Bao) which was published in Nanking. Only then did it come home to me that there were other saints elsewhere who zealously served the Lord. My outlook which had previously been very narrow now began to widen. From 1924 I had a desire to visit Nanking and to enjoy spiritual fellowship with various saints there. In the spring of 1925 I began to send manuscripts to the Spiritual Light Newspaper and began to correspond with some of the believers who had responsibility for the publication. One day in my correspondence I mentioned my idea of visiting Nanking and I then received a letter of welcome. So on May 27th I boarded the train for the south. At 10 o'clock the next evening I arrived at Pugou and crossed the River Yangtze. From there to Nanking I travelled by cart. Sitting on the cart I suddenly realized that I was like a kindergarten child longing to be taught and instructed by God.

A necessary humiliation

Within a few days of arriving in Nanking I met a number of believers whom I had wanted to see for a long time and I was greatly cheered. I also had a number of preaching engagements. At a meeting on June 1st I felt that I should indicate clearly my own beliefs; because of this I was misunderstood by an elderly believer. This aroused further misunderstanding which at the time made me very grieved. Only afterwards did I realize that this was all of God's grace. For when a young man is just beginning his ministry, if everything goes well and he experiences neither opposition nor adversity, he can become proud and overbearing. He can fall into the trap of the Devil. When I first arrived in Nanking I was esteemed and respected by some of the believers there and unconsciously my heart became lifted up with pride. At that juncture came misunderstanding and it was that which brought me down. Otherwise I would have gone on as before and my eventual fall would have been all the greater. God used me; He also disciplined me. 'Blessed is the man whom thou chastenast, O Lord, and teachest him out of they law.' (Psalm 94:12). I remained in Nanking for fourteen days

I remained in Nanking for fourteen days altogether. In the autumn of 1930 the meetings in Peking were placed on a more permanent basis and my work there vastly increased so from that time on I was not able to be absent from Peking more than six months each year.

Practical lessons

During my three visits south of the River Yangtze in 1925 and 1926, apart from engaging in preaching ministry, I also learnt a great deal of a practical nature. I learnt, for instance, about staying in hotels, about receiving a church's hospitality when engaged in ministry, and most of all about staying in the homes of believers. I learnt how to meet different kinds of people, how to deal with a variety of problems. I carefully observed all I saw and took note of details. Based on my experiences I later wrote the booklets 'Practical Lessons for Believers' and 'How to be a kind and tactful Christian'. So I not only discovered a great deal of value to myself, I was also a able to help others.

Grasp of Doctrine

More important than this was the progress I was able to make in my understanding of true doctrine. For while I fulfilled preaching engagements I also continually read my Bible. Book by book and chapter by chapter I gave close attention to the words. When I came across passages that I could not understand I became downcast and interrupted my reading. I assumed that in order to work for God in the future I needed to understand the whole Bible and to be able to explain the whole Bible. That is why I paid special attention to becoming acquainted with the Bible. My participation in the ministry brought a deeper awareness of what was needed in the church and a deeper understanding of the situation in the church. I also saw that what many preachers were distributing to the flock was other than what they needed. My perception gradually changed.

Leading the Flock

I came to appreciate that the greatest need of the flock was not so much for me to understand all the Scriptures but to develop my trust in and dependence on the Word of God to produce the fruits of holiness

and piety and to live a life like Christ. If we do not achieve this, even though we preach the Bible most clearly and even though those who listen are given perfect understanding we shall nurture only Pharisee-type Christians — and that is all. It was beginning to dawn on me that for a Christian to be usable he must first build a firm foundation based on the Bible and he must then go on to seek a pious and holy life. Having done that he must then apply his mind to studying books, to studying events, and to studying people. He must become acquainted with prevalent sins, he must have a deeper understanding of the deceit and depravity in men's hearts, he must become more aware of the needs and suffering of mankind. He must find out more of human feelings.

As I became conscious of all these things I paid more attention to the preaching of repentance toward God and faith in the Lord Jesus Christ. I also placed more emphasis on the life of Christ. For no matter how zealously a Christian prays, no matter how hard he studies his Bible, no matter how regularly he attends meetings, no matter how much he goes around preaching, if he does not live out the life of Christ he will bring to God not glory but dishonour.

At the age of 21 when I began in my home to discipline myself and to read the Bible, at one point I tied up many books and prepared to burn them. I took the view at that time that apart from the Bible no other books were necessary. But after a while I realized that we could read books with benefit to a believer's faith and conduct. While going around preaching I realized that in order to help and counsel people I must first know their needs, their background and their sorrows. I must know how to help them solve their problems. As a result I took the position that we must 'study books, study events, study people'. So for more than 20 years, as I have carried on my work, I have never ceased to learn. And I am still learning. I am aware that the things I don't understand are legion; and there is a great deal yet to be studied. I have never studied at a Theological College but I have been taught in the theological college set up by God. I have not yet graduated.

Further expansion of the ministry

In 1927 my ministry entered a new phase. For in the spring of that year I began to publish 'The Spiritual Food Quarterly' and with increasing commitments outside I became particularly busy.

In the latter part of February I was invited to preach in the three eastern provinces (Manchuria) and I preached in more than ten places in that region. It was my first trip beyond the frontier (Shan-Hai-Gwan). I went to three Lutheran Churches and nine Presbyterian Churches. The number of genuine believers and faithful preachers in that area was painfully small. External activities abounded — with schools, hospitals and so on — but work of a truly spiritual nature was pitiably weak. No sooner had I concluded my meetings and left the area than opposition arose. People said that I tended to criticize and revile people. Yet others acknowledged that the meetings had been a great help to them and the hope was expressed that I would go to the north-east again. Others again were against my being invited back. Be that as it may, churches that had been pervaded by an atmosphere of death were now coming to life.

During June and July I remained in Peking. The weekly meetings in my home and the meetings twice a week in the home of Mrs Pan were then resumed. On September 15th I set out for the north-eastern provinces for the second time. This time I preached at nine centres connected with the Presbyterian Church.

This second visit was longer than the first. This enabled me to deal more fully with important truths. Conditions in the churches were really deplorable. Church members were neither hot nor cold. In a formal way they 'attended worship' but the preachers had no vital message to proclaim to them. Nobody enquired whether these people had sins to be repented of. Nobody gave thought to the relationship of these people to Christ or declared what Christ could do for them. Nobody gave thought to basic beliefs. Yet when the trumpet of God sounded many were awakened. They began to be conscious of their sin and failure; the matter of their relationship to Christ became a vital consideration. Genuinely they began to turn to Christ and to put their trust in Him; they accepted the gift of new life which He offered them.

There were of course others who remained unawakened and who neither changed their attitude nor repented. A natural cleavage arose. In the eyes of those who had not grasped the truth the churches which were normally quiescent had now been blown as by a gale into a state of commotion, and they put the blame for what they saw as confusion on me. On the other hand those who saw God in this were convinced that He had begun a good work in the midst of the churches. Certainly 1927 was a year of transformation for the churches of Manchuria. The division among the preachers was apparent at the Presbyterian Manchurian Synod in the summer. Some were violently opposed to my being invited for ministry again. But it was those in favour — those, in fact, who felt that a further visit was urgently needed — who won the day. That is how it came about that in the autumn I went there once again.

On February 1st, 1928, I accepted an invitation to go and preach at the Presbyterian Church in the west suburb at Baoding. It was now more than seven years since I had been forced to give up my work there. I found that the situation had changed little from what it had been when I left. Even the weather was the same and the ground was covered with a carpet of snow as it had been when I left. Of course when it came to myself I recognized that my whole world had undergone a complete change. There was also a significant difference in my relationship. Whereas I had left in shame and grief I now returned to be welcomed as a preacher. In some ways it was an experience like that of Joseph of old. I was able to minister there for eight days before returning to Peking. How wonderful are the ways of God!

On November 9th (1931) I left Canton for Hongkong . . . on the 19th I took a steamer from Hongkong to Amoy. Amoy is not a large place but I found five 'Many's' — many gambling houses, many opium dens, many pawn-shops, many brothels and many pigeon-ticket shops. You would be right in describing it as a concourse for all kinds of sin and a meeting-place for all kinds of evil.

The city has two places of historical interest. At one of them you see the ruins of a Roman Catholic Church first built there in the 17th century. This great edifice was destroyed by fire many years ago but the front wall and the images are preserved perfectly. A cross on the top of the wall is also undamaged. The date 1602 is inscribed on the base of one of the pillars, so we see that it already has a history of more than 300 years.

In another place you may see the grave of Robert Morrison who was the first Protestant missionary to China; the grave is in the Protestant Cemetery. The grave has a simple head-stone with the inscription 'Robert Morrison, the first Protestant missionary to China.' I returned to Hongkong having preached in Amoy at meetings lasting three days.

(Details are given of extensive itinerant work from 1931-37).

Throughout the years that I have been visiting churches in various locations I have had one particular difficulty. It is that there have been far too many invitations for the time at my disposal. Every year I have published four issues of 'The Spiritual Food Quarterly'. Most of the manuscripts for this have been written during breaks in my ministry in different places. Of course when it came time for the publication I made a point of returning to Peking. I had to oversee the setting up of the type and do the proof-reading.

Although I had several colleagues in the work of the Tabernacle I was still unable to travel too far. There were two relevant factors. Every year I was away on the average about six months. Reckoning the time required by travel as well as in actual ministry this would allow me to visit not more than 20 places in 6 months.

People may sometimes ask me how many people have come to Christ during my more than 20 years ministry in various places. But this is a question I cannot answer. For when I preach the Gospel, wherever it may be, I simply proclaim the words of God to the congregation. Afterwards I leave it to the Spirit of God to use His words to do His own work in people's hearts.

Reflections

The commission that God gave me more than 20 years ago was to preach His word to counter the corruption which is found both in the world and in the church. Looking back over these years I realize that for anyone to exercise important ministries like that is not at all easy. And how much more difficult for me who from my earliest days have had so much regard for 'face' and for fame and glory. By nature I am averse to creating enemies; by nature I am unhappy to be reviled or slandered. By nature I want everybody to respect me, to love me, and to be my friends. My natural desire is to welcome everybody and to eulogize everybody. Yet as a result of seeking to be faithful to God I have to endure the invective, the insults, the slander, and the attacks of many people. And God does not allow me to spare my own 'face' or to consider my own reputation. His call and His commission constrain me. Yet His grace and His power provide a shelter for me. And that is how I can boldly proclaim the message He wants me to proclaim. It is also why I have acquired many friends as well as raised up many enemies. Thank God! What He promised to the prophet Jeremiah is also true for me: 'They shall fight against thee; but they shall not prevail against thee; for I am with thee, saith the Lord, to deliver thee.'

Why did I encounter opposition? Apart from the fact that I rebuked prevalent sins both in the world and in the church, and that I opposed not only false prophets but also the apostate teaching of modernists, there was also another reason. It was that I opposed all traditions in the church that did not harmonize with Scripture. There are some believers who regard these traditions as equal in authority to the Scriptures. The Roman Catholic Church brought in many practices not according to the Bible. At the time of the Reformation in the 15th and 16th centuries not a few of the Roman Catholic doctrines were given up by the Protestant churches, but some of the traditional practices were retained. Now why is it that I personally have not accepted these traditions. It is because when I studied the truth I had not only never studied at a theological college but also I have never studied any theological books. All I did was to read the Old Testament and the New Testament over and over again. My beliefs and the message I preached were derived in their entirety from the Bible. I cared not how many truths some preachers had uprooted from the Bible, nor how many traditions had been added by others, whatever I found in the Bible I accepted — no less and no more. It was not surprising therefore that certain believers both misunderstood me and opposed me.

Temptation

At one stage I passed through a period of temptation when the devil put an unworthy thought in my mind. I reflected on the past. In my travels to various parts of China I had preached to people who could be numbered in tens of thousands. My books were being read throughout the country. Through these activities I had become widely known; and amongst the people who knew me were many who looked up to me and loved me. The thought now occurred to me, Why should I hold on to the policies I have followed in the past and thus continue to arouse opposition, invective, and attack? Suppose I remove from my preaching all those passages that give offence; suppose I cease to teach those doctrines that people regard as myths; suppose I no longer censure apostasy; would I not bring to an end the hostility of those who do not agree with me? By adopting this line I could retain the honour and respect already gained — in fact I would win even greater honour — and I could avoid being misunderstood, opposed, and attacked in the future. I could in fact become an influential and honourable personality in the church. Thank God, I recognized this as being the temptation of the devil. He wanted me to rebel against God, to fall into sin, and to break up the work of God. God also brought to my remembrance the words of Luke 6:26: 'Woe unto you when all men shall speak well of you!'

I was not prepared to be a captive of Satan. Even less did I wish to rebel against God. It was my desire to remain loyal to God to the end. I rejected Satan's temptation. I must continue faithfully preaching the Word of God; I must continue to be a prophet who speaks plainly; and that means that I must continue to endure the persecution which was endured by the prophets of old. God enables me to continue as a fortified city, an iron pillar, and a bronze wall. 'They will fight against you but will not overcome you.'

Wong as a small boy with his mother and sister

1926 Wong with his mother and sister

1925 Miss Liu Jing-Wun at Hangjou

August 1933 on Crouching Tiger Mountain

1936 Baptismal Service

Pulpit of Christians' Tabernacle

"In his prime"

5.
Overseer of the flock...

Take heed therefore unto yourselves and to all the flock,
over which the Holy Ghost hath made you overseers, to
feed the church of God, which he hath purchased with
his own blood.' (Acts 20:28)

These words were addressed by Paul at Miletus to
the elders of the church at Ephesus. He wanted them
to be clear in their minds that although they had been
appointed overseers of the whole flock by the
apostles, yet more important was the fact that they
had been made overseers by the Holy Spirit. Paul gave
them this reminder so that they might recognize the
weight of their responsibility and the importance of
their commission. Therefore they had to be watchful
for themselves and watchful for the whole flock. It is
obvious from this that if those who shepherd the

church have only a human appointment, and are not appointed by the Holy Spirit, then they are basically unqualified to oversee the flock. In all organizations you can have officials appointed by men, but without the guidance and seal of the Holy Spirit you cannot have true leaders in the church. In the churches today there are bishops, elders, pastors and deacons in large numbers. But how many are appointed by the Holy Spirit? And how many are appointed only by men? The Holy Spirit cannot appoint those who have not believed as overseers of the flock. The Holy Spirit cannot appoint those with inconsistent conduct as overseers of the flock. Even less can He appoint those who 'regard piety as a path to profit' as overseers of the flock.

Obviously we cannot say how many church leaders today are appointed by the Holy Spirit and how many are not appointed by the Holy Spirit. But it is quite clear that many occupy offices in the church without being appointed by the Spirit. Why is the church today so corrupt? Naturally there are many reasons for this, but the absence of Spirit-appointed leaders is one of the outstanding reasons. Without good leaders there can be no worthwhile accomplishments. How great is the loss where a church has no faithful leaders! How can there be revival without Spirit-appointed overseers? One of the most important prayers that we can ever pray for the Church is that the Spirit of God will raise up overseers.

At the age of 20 I knew clearly that I was called by God to serve Him. However, I still thought that He wanted me to work within the boundaries of my original denomination. I expected to receive financial help that would enable me to enter a theological college. At the age of 21 God guided me in a particular way and my plan to go to theological college had to be scrapped. Nevertheless I did not lose the impression that God wanted me to reform corrupt practices in the old churches. After two or three years, however, I gradually became convinced that it was basically impossible to do this. One reason for this was that too few of the church members gave evidence of having truly repented and believed. Further, many serving leaders were of the 'regard-piety-as-the-path-to-profit' variety. To talk to people like this about reforming the church was like 'asking a tiger for his skin'. It thus came about that I went less frequently to those particular services and gave more time to searching the Scriptures in my own home. As opportunities arose I talked with others and studied the Bible with them. But I had no intention whatever of starting a new work. The thought never crossed my mind.

The work in Peking

The building of the Christian Tabernacle in Peking was a matter of step-by-step guidance. I referred in the previous chapter to the meetings in my home attended by a handful of people. In the spring of 1933 we rented a hall (the She-chiao Hall) to accommodate our growing numbers. Just at that time my old friend Shih Tien-min and another brother were looking for a place to live. They were favourably impressed by a certain house but their two families did not need all the rooms in it. The thought then occurred to them, why not set aside the large room on the north side of the courtyard as a meeting-place? After discussion and prayer we decided to follow this suggestion. But we had neither chairs nor table. And we had to find money for rent. Previously when we met in the homes of believers the table and chairs and utensils were provided. Moreover there was no rent to pay. And when we hired the She-chiao Hall we placed an offering box inside the hall and the offerings covered expenses.

With our latest move we decided to order 100 forms, each seating three people, and a table for the preacher. We also planned to remove partitions in the room and to cover it with wallpaper. For these expenses and for the rent we would need about 450 dollars (Chinese). I requested the believers to bring their offerings within three weeks to meet these expenses and to place them in the offering box. We decided that after three weeks we would use the money then available to buy chairs, but that on no account would we ask anyone to advance the money. In the event the money contributed amounted to 500 dollars, so we were able to go ahead and buy all the furniture we needed. Our first meeting in this newly-rented accommodation (No 23 Chien-sha-mien Lane) was on April 23, 1933.

The work grows

From that time on we had a comparatively convenient meeting-place. If we crowded in a little we could seat 180 to 200 people, and in the courtyard we could seat another 100 people. We could also seat another 20 or 30 in the rooms rented by three families of believers. So altogether we could accommodate more than 300 people. The first group to be baptized were baptized on June 10th in the river outside the west suburbs. They were six in number. And beginning that summer we arranged an annual convention lasting more than 10 days. Every year I made three preaching trips away from Peking and they took up roughly half the year. While I was away the work in Peking was in the hands of my long-standing friend Shih Tien-min and two other brothers.

Practical difficulties

For a while we were comparatively comfortable and generally happy in our new accommodation. But then we became aware of certain difficulties. In the winter, for instance, it was too cold for us to use the courtyard very long, and yet the rooms would not accommodate all those attending. It was an impasse. All that we could do was to urge those wearing warm clothes to sit outside and to allow those with thinner clothes to sit inside the rooms. When I made an announcement to this effect some people were truly gracious; they had come early and were seated inside, but they readily went outside and allowed others to take their places inside.

In 1934 we commenced an eight days evangelistic campaign on February 14th, taking advantage of the fact that it was a general holiday. We put up a tent in the courtyard like the kind of tent used for weddings. We made two heating stoves with bricks. Naturally it was not as warm as inside the rooms but it was certainly warmer than in the open air. Evangelistic meetings were held in this fashion every spring. As soon as the weather became warmer we moved the windows so that the interior of the rooms and the courtyard outside were linked together. In this way those in the courtyard could not only hear the sermon they could also see the preacher. The preacher, on his side, could also see the people in the courtyard. But when the weather became cold again we had to replace the windows.

On August 1st in 1934 we opened our second summer convention scheduled for 14 days. On the evening of August 8th, just as I was about to start preaching, a heavy downpour of rain engulfed us. The members of the congregation in the courtyard leapt to their feet to find shelter from the rain. But the rooms were already full. A few managed to squeeze into the meeting-room. Others found shelter in the rooms belonging to the families of the believers on the east, west and south sides of the courtyard. The few who remained sought whatever shelter they could get under the eaves, but their clothes were soaked. Such an experience brought the realization that we could not continue to meet there indefinitely. We needed a building even more suitable than that. And for this I then began to pray.

Not many days had passed before God put a thought in my heart. It was that we should buy a plot of land and erect our own building. I prayed over this idea for several days and I discussed it with like-minded fellow believers. As a result I prepared another offering-box specifically for the erection of a new building. I announced this to the congregation and invited all who wished to contribute to put their offerings in the box whenever we had a meeting. We also selected five believers to take charge of these funds. As soon as funds were sufficient we would go ahead and buy land.

By the spring of 1936 we had more than 2,000 dollars in hand. The time had come to look for a plot of land. In March we went to see a house in Shih-Jia Hutong. (Hutong = a lane or side street in places where there have been Manchus) and immediately I saw it I said to myself, 'This place is ideal; buy it.'

However, some of the believers advised us to look at other places in the hope of finding a place with a more suitable price. We did this. But in spite of expending much time and strength we found nothing more suitable.

New premises

From the outset we had decided on several principles. First, not to buy property on a street designated with the name of an idol or temple . . . Second, the location should be near the centre of the city so that none of the believers, no matter where situated would need to travel too far. Third, the location should be near a main street where it would be easy to find. For one thing this would obviate newcomers having to waste time looking for us, and for another the approach would not be unduly muddy at times of rain or snow. No 42 Shih-Jia Lane was ideal on all three counts. We decided to buy it. In April we came to an understanding with the owner though at that time we only had about 3,000 dollars in hand. A little more time was needed for the owner to get his papers ready and by the time he had done this we had received enough to make the purchase. (The house was demolished to provide a building site). In October we also bought some vacant land in front of the Ministry of Finance.

During the period that we had been preparing to buy land and put up a building I had given some thought to the question of registering with the government, for when a church buys land it is supposed to use the name of the group on the deeds. Moreover, when eventually the hall was completed we should need a proper designation. After many days of prayer and consideration I chose 'The Christians' Tabernacle' (lit. the Christians' Assembly Hall) as our designation.

On February 8th we received notification from the police that we could proceed with registration and on March 5th we completed registration with the Social Affairs Bureau. On March 21st we hung a notice board with white background and black ideographs outside the main gate of the Tabernacle. On it was written the words 'Christians' Tabernacle'. This was our official designation.

A new building

By the spring of 1937 we had several thousand dollars in our hands and we began preparations to build a hall. A certain contractor estimated that a hall seating 450 people would cost more than 20,000 dollars. At the time we dare not think in terms of anything stylish; all we hoped for was a 'solid tent' that would not collapse when buffeted by wind and rain. With that we could be content. But God's thoughts are higher than our thoughts for during the spring and summer of that year we built a slate-roofed building for worship, 70 feet long and 40 feet wide, for a cost of 6,792 dollars. Work began at the beginning of May; it was finished before the end of July.

Before the work had started I was one day invited to have a chat with a sister who had been ill and confined to her bed for a long time. She enquired about arrangements for heating in winter and asked whether it was feasible to lay pipes for hot air. She remarked that coal stoves would not be aesthetically attractive and that with them you had the problem of ashes. Furthermore they would occupy the space of several seats. Our sister then explained that if I did not oppose the use of hot air pipes she would be happy to present to us the whole installation. Before that time we had never dared to think of central heating being installed. But God was providing it for us which was far beyond all that we had thought. How great is His grace!

It happened that hostilities between Japan and China broke out at that time (with the incident at nearby Marco Polo Bridge on July 7th, 1937). The new hall at 42 Shih-Jia Lane was completed by the end of July and on August 1st a dedication service was held attended by about 500 people. A day or two earlier, on July 28th, the Chinese army had withdrawn. The Japanese army entered the city on August 8th. Because people's hearts were full of fear and because business in the city had come to a standstill our summer convention was extended and lasted altogether 18 days.

(Incidentally the translator of this book arrived in Peking from the interior on the way to attend a wedding in Tienjin just before the Marco Polo Bridge incident. The spread of fighting necessitated a return by another route.)

Fighting spread through North China and Central China with the inevitable consequence that all communications were broken. Meetings which I had arranged to lead during the latter part of the year had to be cancelled and I remained in Peking. People's hearts were restless and fearful and I saw it as God's perfect will that I should be on hand.

My work outside Peking continued to be restricted. A frontier formed itself between the area occupied by the Japanese Army and the area of Free China. People used all means possible to cross from one side to the other, but for my part I could not tell lies in order to cross over even for the work of the Lord. This meant that I could only operate in occupied territory. Mr Wong's experiences during the occupation of Peking by the Japanese are described in Chapter 10.

Everyone was happy that we could have a hall. We were protected alike from the fierce heat of summer and from the freezing winds of winter. In addition we no longer needed to worry lest the seats were insufficient. In 1938 we added a small upstairs room on the south side of the courtyard.

The equipment and furnishings inside the hall were marked by simplicity, cleanliness and dignity. The walls were as white as snow and no words or pictures were hung on them. This was so that nothing should distract the attention of the worshippers and so that they could worship God with singleness of heart. Neither outside the building nor inside did we have a cross, for that is the mark of the Roman Catholic Church. A white stone on the south-east corner outside carries an inscription of four sentences which indicate our faith and the truths we emphasize. There is also the date when the building was erected. These are the sentences:

He was wounded for our transgressions.
He rose again from among the dead.
He has already been received into heaven.
He will come again to receive us.

In order to economize in space our pulpit was made very small, less than 12 feet long and less than 7 feet broad — just big enough to place a table and two or three chairs and a blackboard. In front of the pulpit is a baptistry and on each side of the baptistry there are curtains which can be drawn for use at times of baptisms.

By the spring of 1946 I had recovered my health almost completely, but because I had left my bed too early my knee was still painful and is painful even now.

In the winter of 1945 I received letters from a number of places in the province of Szechwan and in March I took a plane to Chongking. From there I went on to Chungdu where I conducted a number of evangelistic meetings for university students. I also led meetings for believers.

I returned to Peking just as my sister became ill, and within a few days my mother also became ill. My mother gradually recovered but my sister's illness became more serious and she passed away on September 1st. This was a great grief to my mother, who was elderly and physically weak, and she could not leave me. So for the time being I confined my activities to Peking. Apart from accepting invitations to go to Tienjin I did not go away to take meetings.

Then Mrs Pan, with whom we had had fellowship in the Lord for 23½ years also became ill and passed away on the 27th. I was invited to lead the funeral service. This devout lady had not only had a great deal to do with my work over the past years, she also left an impression on my spirit and on my life which could never be erased. 'She being dead yet speaks'.

Throughout that year the work in Peking was unprecedentedly heavy. When fighting (with the Communists) broke out in the suburbs in December, people's hearts were even more troubled and fearful, and stood in need of strength and comfort. So not only was it more difficult for me to engage in travel it was also more necessary for me to remain with the believers.

Pastoral principles
We are very strict in receiving believers. Unless we

are quite sure that a person has repented and believed in the Lord and is thereby saved we will on no account accept him for baptism. We do not enquire into knowledge of doctrine, we only emphasize repentance, faith, and salvation. This experience must be evidenced by the change in their manner of life. In some cases it is soon clear that they have repented and believed, and they can be baptized without delay. In other cases it is more difficult to be sure. We then ask them to wait; it may be a year, or two years, or even three years, and only then can they be baptized. In some cases they are asked to wait so long that they begin to complain and even grow angry. They cease to attend meetings. It is certainly well that such people have been delayed, for if they became church members it would not be for the good of the church. On the other hand some people when asked to wait will show no sign of complaint or anger; they remain humble and they diligently attend meetings. They acknowledge that God's time has not yet come, and when they are baptized eventually they are usually good Christians.

We are sometimes slandered by those who do not understand what we are doing. They charge us with enticing believers from other churches to join our church. In actual fact it is not that we entice people to join us, it is that they themselves come and ask to join us, and we do not make it at all easy for them to do so. Experience has taught us that the reason why some Christians leave their original church and seek to join another one is not always because they love the truth. Some may have fallen into sin and have been disciplined in their own church. It may be that their objective was to gain fame and wealth and that they have failed in their objective. They think of nothing but revenge. People like this only join another church so that they have the means to attack the church they have left. Consequently we are particularly careful and we do not lightly accept believers from other churches.

Looking back over the years I recall many cases where newly formed churches have criticized older churches and they have tried to entice believers in the older churches to join them. Yet within ten or twenty years the conditions in the newer churches are worse than those in the churches they criticized. I have seen this phenomenon and have been warned; I will on no account follow this pattern. I am unwilling to work with wood, hay, and stubble. These things appear to be all right but not one of them will survive the fire. What I want to work with is gold, silver and precious stones. These things although very small will endure. To accept three 'truly believing Christians' is better than to receive three hundred or three thousand church members who have no life. We are not interested in fame or gain that is based on numbers, and since we are not interested in increasing our own prestige, why should we entice people to join us? I know for a fact, however, that there are preachers who certainly act in this way. Those who do not know me tend to put me in the same category, and how can I blame them?

During the past 17 years not more than about 570 believers have been baptized here altogether. Yet many newly formed churches have had as many baptisms as this within the first two years. Sometimes we have had not more than one or two baptized at one time, sometimes up to ten or more, and on one occasion twenty. But I sometimes see churches baptize as many as 200 at one time and I am anxious for them. Originally we received people fairly easily, but in recent years I have learnt through bitter experience to be stricter.

There are no salaried workers in our church. But the believers always remember those who work for God. As led by the Holy Spirit they make their contributions to the workers. It is to God they make their offerings and God's workers receive what they need from Him. Inside each door of our meeting hall we have placed an offering box and believers put in their offerings at each meeting. If their offering is for a servant of God they put it in an envelope appropriately designated. Those not designated are used for general expenses. All our income is derived from the offering boxes. We do not use a bag to receive offerings since, on the one hand, it may make unbelievers feel that in order to hear the message they must pay money, and on the other hand it may put believers with limited resources in an embarrassing position.

Qualifications for workers

When we choose believers to take responsibility for different kinds of work in the church, what we emphasize most of all is their beliefs and their integrity. Gifts and power and knowledge and learning are all placed second. As regards people's wealth and possessions we pay no attention at all. I have observed many churches when choosing people to take positions of responsibility look for wealth and possessions. So long as a believer has wealth he is held in high esteem. The people exalt him; they invite him to take responsibility; they choose him to be a leader. Their ultimate objective is for the church to benefit from his wealth. But as soon as a church sets out along a path like this it incurs spiritual disgrace, it becomes corrupt, and it collapses. Their mode of action may be likened to Israel's worshipping the golden calf. I frequently observe this grievous and lamentable phenomenon. Therefore I particularly guard against this danger. When someone who is wealthy or who has a high position becomes a Christian, he should not soon be appointed to take responsibility. Men like this need to be disciplined by God in a particular way. For owing to their wealth and fame they have been esteemed and respected in society, and this may have made them proud and arrogant, and that is something repugnant to God. After they become Christians, even though other believers do not eulogize them it is still difficult for them to avoid a feeling of superiority. They should therefore be dealt with exactly as others are dealt with so that it is brought home to them that in the sight of God they are not a whit better than others. As time goes on, as their proud and arrogant attitude gradually disappears, they can then — and only then — be given positions of responsibility.

It is unfortunately true that, in the majority of churches, as soon as the members see people with wealth or position become Christians they seek to ingratiate themselves in various ways and strive to please them, according them places of special honour. They hope in this way to secure the help of men like this and to attract their financial contributions.

May I ask you a question? Think of all the elders, deacons, board members, and committee members in the church who are known to you and tell me how many of them are without social standing or without money. With my own eyes I have seen people of questionable character and of bad reputation being flattered and held in esteem; they are made church leaders and given positions of authority. In faith and virtue and knowledge they are in no way superior to others. The only things special about them is that they have money and standing. Can a church with leaders like this be other than corrupted? Can it avoid becoming a nest for the devil?

Without question we have lost not a few people from our church simply because we refuse to exalt those who in society have riches and standing. It sometimes happens that people of this type, on believing in the Lord, expect to be given a special standing in the church. When they do not receive it they become dissatisfied. They then remove themselves to other churches where they are given the honour which they think is their due.

There are also some who come to us by transfer from other churches where they have enjoyed honour commensurate with their position in society. They expect to be honoured in our church in the same way, but when they are accorded no special favour they then find another church where their wealth and standing are recognized. They are treated like rarities and often invited to become leaders in the church. They naturally stay there and do not return to us.

In view of all this it is not surprising that throughout the past ten years or so, although we have had people of affluence and influence attending our meetings, not many of them have stayed with us. Some onlookers would regard this as our church's loss but in actual fact it is our gain. For where you have people who love vain-glory in a church it means a very great handicap for the church.

An emphasis on godly behaviour

There are two strong emphases in my ministry. On the one hand I emphasize beliefs; on the other hand I emphasize the Christian's manner of life. On the one hand I expound the basic truths of the Bible; on the other hand I preach the teaching of the Bible. In every church there are believers who know well the basic truths of the Bible while they fall far short in their conduct — they exhibit pride, love of fame, vanity, lying, covetousness, impurity, envy, hatred, slander, self-seeking, party spirit, and so on. In a situation like this I emphasize the practical aspects of the Christian life. Some people criticize me for stressing conduct and for not stressing faith and grace. But their criticism is invalid. I certainly emphasize faith and as a result I also emphasize conduct. Read what the Scriptures have to say:

'And beside this, giving all diligence, add to your faith virtue; and to virtue knowledge; and to knowledge temperance; and to temperance patience; and to patience godliness; and to godliness brotherly kindness; and to brotherly kindness charity.' (2 Peter 1: 5-7).

'I therefore, the prisoner of the Lord, beseech you that ye walk worthy of the vocation wherewith ye are called.' (Esphesians 4:1).

I am not surprised that many preachers never emphasize conduct and manner of life; it is because their own life falls short in these respects. But to teach these things is not only a help to the hearers it is also a help to the preacher. From the time I believed, when I was 14 years old, I gave full attention to Christian conduct and character. And then, when I began to preach, I preached on Christian conduct just as I preached on Christian faith. I felt, moreover, that I should preach this until the day that I render account to the Lord. A person with a blemished character is a person unworthy to work for God.

At the time I believed on the Lord I received very great help from a friend because he did not hesitate to reprove me and correct me, and through this he laid solid foundations in the making of a man. That is one reason why I deal today in the same way with those whom God has committed to my care and with those who are willing to listen to me. Whenever I see Christians offend against the truth, whether in their actions or in their words, I will on no account lightly let it pass. I do not hesitate to reprove them for their faults and to urge them to repent. This applies to things of little consequence as well as to things of importance. For I am well aware that many big sins arise from little sins.

I also know well that the greatest responsibility of church leaders is to guide believers far away from sin and to help them to tread the path of holiness. This is far more important than merely getting a head knowledge of the contents of the Bible. If a church leader observes believers falling into sins, and if he fails to reprove or warn them, he then becomes a participator in their sins. I dare not ignore what God has entrusted to me; but even less am I willing to share the transgressions of other people.

As I have said, when I reprove and warn others I

not only hope to help those in question, I also help myself. For the more I exhort others the more I need to give heed to myself. Otherwise I have no authority or 'face' to continue such a ministry.

As Paul wrote to the Thessalonians, 'Ye are witnesses, and God also, how holily and justly and unblameably we behaved ourselves among you that believe' (1 Thess. 2:10). Whenever I read these words of Paul I aspire to be that kind of preacher. For it is only this kind of preacher who has authority and power; or who can be an example for other believers. For it does not matter how well men can preach, it does not matter how strong is their appeal, it does not matter how active they are, it does not matter how good they are at public relations – if they fall short in their standards of conduct their work can only flourish briefly. For sooner or later the fact will become evident that their teaching and their conduct do not agree, and they become stumbling-blocks.

Since I do not tolerate sin I have acquired many friends; I have also acquired enemies. Those who are helped by accepting my warnings grow to love me; but those who are unwilling to repent grow to fear me and hate me. If a believer in our fellowship falls into sin there are only two courses before him: one is to confess his sin and repent; the other is to leave us.

No compromise on doctrine

For those who shepherd a church there is another matter of considerable importance. It has to do with distinguishing between truth and error. Church leaders must on no account compromise with error; and not even by a hair's breadth must they tolerate deviation from the truth. Truth must be dealt with positively;

that which is contrary to truth must be firmly rejected. In pursuing this policy we must have no fear of misunderstanding, opposition, attack or persecution. When church leaders become so concerned about feelings and 'face', or so afraid of giving offence, or so fearful of being misunderstood and opposed, or so apprehensive of persecution and danger that they compromise in matters of truth or even deviate from the truth, they will surely lose their authority and power. The church also will begin to deteriorate. God's workmen must be steadfast and courageous. If you would be a faithful servant you must entirely disregard reputation, and in the last analysis you must entirely disregard life.

Excessive fear means surrender to sin or compromise with Satan. Leaders in the church must not only be devout, they must also be courageous. Leaders in the church are like leaders in the army. If leaders in the army are timid, if they flee when approaching the battle-line, or if they lay down their arms before the enemy, then the whole army will forfeit victory. My own natural disposition is to be cowardly, but when God gives me His Word His power overshadows me. Praise be to His Name!

In the activities of our church we have no regard for 'favour' and no regard for 'social standing'. When I receive a request, if I can respond to it I do so, but if I cannot respond to it I decline. Suppose a married couple come to me and ask to be baptized. If I discover that one only is ready for baptism I assent only to that one. I cannot accept both of them simply because they are a married couple. And suppose two friends come to me and ask me to be their guarantor. If only one of the two is known to me then I will be guarantor for that one only and not for both. And suppose an affianced couple ask me to marry them. If for any reason I cannot do this for one of the two I cannot relax on account of the other. 'But let your communication be, yea, yea; nay, nay; for whatsoever is more than these cometh of evil.' (Matthew 5: 37).

Pastoral care

From my experiences over the years I have come to understand that shepherding the church is no easy task. Although the believers meet in one place they are in fact different in nature, different in knowledge, different in viewpoint, different in background. Believers all have the life of Christ but each one still has the flesh and the evils of the flesh. So long as they encounter no particular incident, and so long as they are not shut up together for a long time, no particular difficulty arises. But whenever an incident occurs, or if they are thrown together for a long time in one place, then disagreements arise one after the other.

Some people are slapdash; others are precise and watchful. Some are narrow in heart; others are magnanimous and broad. Some are deceitful and secretive; others are straightforward and sincere. Some are full of suspicions and doubts; some are open and frank. Some preserve their wealth like their life; others scatter money like soil. Some are timid; others are fearless like tigers. Some are self-seeking; others are keen to help others. Furthermore even those with many excellencies still have their shortcomings. There is no such thing as a person with only good points and no shortcomings. Now gather a group of people together with all their differences and as time goes on it is virtually impossible to avoid friction.

These are the people whom the shepherd must guide. When friction arises between them he must strive to bring them to agreement. He must act very carefully or he may make matters worse. For each party sees only its own side of the argument and they may both regard the shepherd as prejudiced and so misunderstand him. There are times when out of deep love and compassion you try to help people, but if what you counsel fails, even in the slightest, to meet the wishes of one or another, then far from being grateful they may even regard you as an enemy. Parents with only a few children sometimes suffer pain like this. What of a shepherd who has several hundred believers in his care?

The reception of believers is another source of misunderstanding. Some people feel that once a person has believed in the Lord then he or she should be allowed to be baptized as soon as possible. What they do not realize, however, is that while some people make profession with their lips, they have not really believed in their heart. There are those who make profession in order to benefit materially. There are some who do so to please their employer or manager. Some make profession of faith because they are interested in a certain person of the opposite sex. There are some who blindly follow others.

Many years ago I also took the view that those who made profession of faith were true believers. After many years of painful experience I have come to the conclusion that, of those who profess to believe in the Lord, less than half have really done so. If you accept indiscriminately all who make profession you are sowing the seeds of serious trouble in the future. How can the church be other than corrupted?

A few years ago there was an extremely zealous but inadequately experienced believer who made great efforts to persuade people to believe in the Lord and, on their profession, to persuade them to be baptized. She brought many people to me to ask for baptism. But after I had talked to these people I discovered that most of them, when it came to the point, had neither faith nor spiritual life. Some of them had found it difficult to resist her pressure and for reasons of 'face' had responded superficially. Naturally I could not agree to their being baptized. As a result the zealous believer was greatly upset. She had worked hard to get people to ask for baptism and she found my reluctance to baptize them hard to bear. So she took them off to another church and within a short time they were all baptized. There are those in our own fellowship who feel that I am unduly careful in this, but I am very clear in my own mind that unless we give careful attention to this matter we shall not protect the church from adulteration.

Protecting the pulpit

Then there is the matter of those who occupy the pulpit. I am extremely careful about this and I never lightly invite anyone outside to preach. This also is a cause of misunderstanding. Apart from my immediate fellow-workers very few have been invited to preach in our pulpit. Suppose we invite preachers without being fully aware of their beliefs, and suppose they proceed to give teaching contrary to the truth, what are we to do? Do we stop them half-way? Or let them finish? Naturally, since I have invited them to preach, it would cause embarrassment for me to stop them half-way. Yet to allow them to finish would harm the hearers. Thus one would be faced with a dilemma. The safest way is never to invite a preacher unless you are fully aware of his beliefs.

There is another reason. Some men are well able to preach but their manner of life is unworthy of a Christian. Unless you are acquainted with a person for some time it is difficult to really know him. Suppose we prematurely invite a man to occupy the pulpit and then later it is found that he has a bad reputation, it means that we have contaminated the sacred pulpit and given a wrong impression to the congregation. In my own experience I have known people engage in preaching when their heart is full of deceit, covetousness, lewdness, envy, pride and selfishness. The pulpit gives them an opportunity to show themselves off, to deceive the congregation, and to entice people to follow them. If harm results through such a preacher then those who invited him cannot disclaim responsibility.

It is indeed a fact that many believers have been adversely affected through the church inviting unsuitable preachers, and in view of this I must be specially careful. But the majority of believers have no experience of this kind and it is extremely difficult for them to realize that those who are gifted as preachers can at the same time be dissolute in their conduct. They think that if a man preaches well he must be God's faithful servant, and they hope that I will invite him to preach at our church. My reluctance to invite someone not known to me is the cause of misunderstanding and criticism. I do not blame them in the least. Over twenty years ago I was the same as they are today. But since then my experience helps me to understand the words with which the Lord Jesus warned His disciples:

"Beware of false prophets, which come to you in sheep's clothing, but inwardly they are ravening wolves. Ye shall know them by their fruits . . . Not everyone that saith unto me, 'Lord, Lord,' shall enter into the kingdom of heaven; but he that doeth the will of my Father which is in heaven. Many will say to me in that day, 'Lord, Lord, have we not prophesied in thy name and in thy name have cast out devils and in thy name done many wonderful works?' And then will I profess unto them, I never knew you: depart from me, ye that work iniquity." (Matthew 7: 15-23).

In the past I have been not a little misunderstood through my reluctance to invite certain preachers. But after the bad reputation of these men had come to light those believers who had misunderstood me have come to see that I was right.

A balanced diet

Zealous believers are deeply concerned about the affairs of the church. They have certain opinions which they hope will be accepted by the preacher and they are greatly disappointed if he does not emphasize them. A shepherd should commend these people for their concern but not necessarily accept their suggestions. In this situation lies a problem. Some believers emphasize a particular aspect of truth and they want to hear it emphasized in the pulpit, just as a person who likes chicken, duck, fish or meat would prefer to eat chicken, duck, fish or meat at every meal, and a person who likes greens or carrots or turnips would prefer to eat greens or carrots or turnips at every meal. Yet intelligent parents would not provide the same food for their children to eat at every meal. That would be a sure way to ruin their health and to hinder their development. Parents must provide a wide variety of food for their children. Likewise the shepherd of a church who is loyal to God and who loves his flock must provide what the believers really need rather than what a few of them want.

Advice to pastors

In view of all these difficulties what ought a shepherd to do and what attitude ought he to adopt? First, he must set himself to understand and to do the will of God. Second, he must preserve an attitude of love towards his flock like the attitude of parents towards their children. Third, he should put right out of his mind all issues of gain or loss, of glory or shame, of benefit or harm, of advantage or disadvantage. Fourth, he ought to preserve an attitude of humility and keep his mind open to instruction. Fifth, he ought to eschew all matters of 'face', not fearing opposition or misunderstanding. These then are pointers to being a worker after God's own heart. Inevitably one who serves God faithfully will face hardships and suffering. But the joy God gives and the reward He promises will recompense him for all.

I myself have been especially favoured by God in that for a period of more than twenty years I have been able to visit several hundred churches. I have noted both the good points and the bad points. I have seen their achievements and their losses, their successes and their failures. I have learned of ways in which upright people have been taken in and of ways in which cunning people deceive others. I have seen how sincere believers have been understood and attacked for a while but how God has brought them to a place of abundance. I have seen many crafty people temporarily obtain power and prosperity but I have also seen how eventually they brought grief upon themselves. I have seen leaders characterized by humility whom God has used greatly and I have seen leaders who are pompous and conceited, proud and overbearing, whom God cast off. I have seen workers for God, strong and courageous, who overcame the threats and terror of the enemy to perform valiantly, and I have seen others, timid and fearful, who have surrendered to brute force and have ended in failure. I have seen holy and incorruptible preachers who have been exalted by God and respected by men, and I have seen covetous and licentious preachers who incurred the displeasure of God. In all this I have taken the faithful as my pattern and the unworthy as my warning.

It is now nearly 25 years since meetings began in my home. From home meetings we moved to rented accommodation and from rented accommodation we moved to a hall that we had built. From a handful of people we gradually progressed to a membership of several hundred. We began in fact with two of us — my friend Shih Tien-min and myself. Much of this development was quite outside my own planning. It is entirely the work of God and it is He who should be praised and worshipped.

I have no desire to do something great. It is simply my hope, in this world where truth is beclouded and where the lusts of men have broken their banks, to be able to testify to God's truth and to live out His life. I wanted to be faithful unto death; in my own particular sphere I want to glorify God; and I want to spread the fragrance of Christ wherever I go. It is not so much a large church that I want to build; it is rather to build up a church according to the mind of

God. Two needs stand out in the world today. One is for model believers; the other is for model churches. My prayer, accordingly, is that we may be model believers, and that ours may be a model church.

December, 1949

6.
Give them some- thing to eat...

Mark 6: 34-44. 'And Jesus, when he came out saw much people, and was moved with compassion toward them, because they were as sheep not having a shepherd . . . And when the day was now far spent, His disciples came unto Him, and said 'This is a desert place, and now the time is far passed: send them away, that they may go into the country roundabout and into the villages, and buy themselves bread: for they have nothing to eat.' He answered and said unto them, 'Give ye them to eat' . . .

This was not a case of the Lord being ignorant that the disciples did not have enough food to distribute among several thousand people. Even less was He ignorant that He alone had the resources to feed so many. What He wanted was to give His disciples a share in this great and glorious task. Consequently, before He performed this stupendous miracle, He issued this order to His disciples: 'Give ye them to eat!'

Did the disciples possess food to distribute to the people? Yes, they did. Although the five loaves and two fishes were in themselves totally inadequate, all that the disciples needed to do was to hand them over to the Lord. Small as the offering was, the Lord could use it to perform a mighty work. Five thousand men ate to the full and even then they could collect twelve baskets full of crumbs.

When I was in my twenty-first year I was especially enlightened by the Lord. I became very zealous for the Way of the Lord. There was an impulse within me that made me want to tell others of the grace I had received. But in various church publications that came into my hands I found articles that were contrary to both Scripture and Truth. I was deeply grieved. It was as if a fire burned within me. It vexed me that I was unable immediately to write and publish articles making a stand for the Truth — to distribute these articles and to warn believers against these erroneous teachings. My heart was burdened because I had the will but not the strength. All I could do was to cry in my anguish, 'Why is there no remedy?'

A gradual development

But the Lord was gracious to me and by 1925 I had a little strength in the matter of finance. As already indicated I then published four booklets and further editions were called for. This was the beginning of my literary work.

I have also described how in 1923 I began to subscribe to the Ling Gwong Bao (Spiritual Light

Newspaper) which was published bi-monthly in Nanking. I was most happy that a magazine of this kind was available for the churches in China. During 1925 I submitted several articles to 'Spiritual Light' all of which were published. Alas! Because of the misunderstanding which arose during my stay in Nanking during June (see Chapter 4) the manuscript that I sent in the summer was returned to me. At the time I was deeply disappointed but afterwards I saw God's gracious purpose in this. For without that experience I would not have considered being involved in the publication of a regular magazine myself. 'Spiritual Light', incidentally, ceased publication in 1927.

During the latter part of 1925 and during 1926 I ministered extensively in the two provinces Jejiang and Jiangsu. Believers asked me repeatedly to mimeograph my messages so that they could either keep them or pass them on. But because I was greatly pressed for time I had to hold back. However, I turned the matter over in my mind, and it occurred to me that it would be better to produce a publication for believers all over the country than have separate local printings. At first I still dare not think in terms of a regular magazine. But I knew that inertia was a strong feature in my make up, and I realized that unless I decided on a regular publication I would accomplish little. I recorded the following in my diary dated October 28, 1926 at Sujou after a lapse of 13 days: 'This afternoon, having thought and prayed over the proposed publication, I got the name "Spiritual Food Quarterly" (Ling-Shih-Ji-Kan)."

The title 'Spiritual Food Quarterly' is based, of course, on the words of the Lord Jesus, 'Give them something to eat!' Wherever I have travelled I have seen people needing spiritual food just as the multitude of more than 5,000 people needed material food. I heard in my spirit the voice of the Lord, 'Give them something to eat!' It was a commission I dare not refuse. I was also happy to accept it. I was quite willing to take my loaves and my fishes and to hand them over to the Lord. He could use them in any way He wanted and they could be distributed to the multitude. The Lord is truly faithful and compassionate. He accepted our tiny offering and during the 20 years that we have distributed this insignificant spiritual food we have reached not 5,000 but upwards of 50,000. Even I who made the offering have been blessed and edified far beyond my expectation.

Towards the end of 1926 I returned from Jejiang and Jiangsu to Peking. In January 1927 I spent much time in prayer and thought as we prepared for the publication of this new magazine. I regarded it as a highly important work but I still feared to act precipitately. I was therefore careful and careful again . . .

On January 12th I went to the Peking Post Office Administration Bureau to enquire about the registration of magazines. Only then did I discover that we must first get a licence from the Police Bureau. I had heard that this process was particularly troublesome and since I was ignorant of the processes involved I went to the Police Bureau with some misgivings. However we were able to move ahead without some of the complications I had anticipated. When I learnt that publishing a magazine would require a guarantor, one of the Christians on his own initiative went ahead and found one. On January 17th we satisfactorily completed our negotiations with the printer. We now only awaited police approval.

Earlier, when we first made plans for the publication of 'Spiritual Food', I myself had put down 150 dollars to meet expenses. So when we filled in the application form at the Police Bureau I entered the capital as 150 dollars. On January 29th the Police Bureau sent a representative to examine us and he explained that the capital for a magazine must be at least 200 dollars. In view of this I gave another 50 dollars.

While we awaited the necessary authorization from the Police Bureau I prepared all the needed articles for the first issue. I had already accepted invitations to visit several places in the north-east (Manchuria), but because we were still awaiting approval for the Quarterly I delayed a little. Finally, because there was still no word of any kind from the Police Bureau I could delay no longer and on February 24th set out to cross the border.

This itinerary was to include more than ten places and to last two or three months. But on March 8th I heard from Peking that the licence for the publication of 'The Spiritual Food Quarterly' had now been received. Since my long-standing friend Shih Tien-Min was the only one available in Peking to take responsibility (in addition to his duties as a school teacher) I had to go back to Peking for a while and I returned to the north-east on April 1st. The first issue of 'The Spiritual Food Quarterly' appeared during the latter part of April. Since then this small publication has gone all over the world.

The first editorial

In the first issue of the Quarterly I wrote an introductory article which contained the following:

"Mankind was created by God and given life. But in order to preserve life and to be capable of growth a man depends on nourishment. To develop from the weakness of infancy to the strength of manhood he requires food. When food is adequate we are healthy and strong; when food is inadequate we are weak and sickly. Thus when God created man He first prepared for him an abundance of food. This is what He said: 'Behold, I have given you every herb bearing seed, which is upon the face of all the earth, and every tree, in the which is the fruit of a tree yielding seed; to you it shall be for meat.' (Genesis 1:29) . . .

The food that God first prepared was material food; the food that He provided later was spiritual. Material food can help man to grow, but in the end it cannot save him from frailty and death. Spiritual food, on the other hand, can give man new life in the present and secure for him an eternal inheritance.

Alas! Although the food that God has prepared is so abundant there are still many people who have not received even a little. Obviously there are some people who are unwilling to receive it; they have not yet appreciated its importance. People like this are to be pitied. But there are many others who have heard and believed; they have experienced salvation. But they are satisfied with themselves and make no further progress. It is as if a child is treated as a grown man immediately it is born. He can be left to himself. But in reality a child that receives no nourishment will neither remain healthy nor grow.

There are Christians who have believed for many years. Yet they still want to feed on milk. Only barely do they survive, being content with a minimum of teaching. Why don't they seek the food that is rich in nutriment? It is true that they have not wasted away, yet they are far from attaining their full growth in Christ. They have not reached that point in their experience that God wants them to reach.

The crowd that followed Jesus and listened to His word lacked material food. Yet the Lord Jesus had pity on them. Will not Jesus manifest His compassion today for those who lack spiritual food? As then, so now. The voice of the Lord Jesus sounds in our ears: 'Give them something to eat!'

Do you remember the words of the Lord Jesus to His disciples? 'Who then is that faithful and wise steward, whom his lord shall make ruler over his household, to give them their portion of meat in due season?' (Luke 12:42).

Whenever I read this passage I can only sigh and lament. For although stewards are numerous there are very very few who can distribute the food according to the needs. We have philosophic argument, tedious lectures, the uplift of character, the reformation of society, the spirit of sacrifice — and these things may indeed have a modicum of usefulness; but for the basic needs of the human heart they are but chaff and dust. How can they nourish the hungry to make them strong and to help them to grow? Alas, most of the things distributed from our pulpits and from Christian publications are only of minor importance.

There is another circumstance that causes us even greater grief. It is that many unbelieving leaders in the churches are openly serving harmful things to their people. What do they say? They say, 'The Christian way of life consists of service and sacrifice. Jesus is the highest pattern of personality. He is the reformer of dark society . . . Depending on the spread of learning the world will be reconstructed to become heaven. The virgin birth of Christ, His atonement, resurrection and return are myths. The Bible is no more than a history of the Hebrew religion, and not all of it is to be believed.'

Distortions of this kind are like yeast and spread their corrupt influence very quickly. Many Christians have already been seriously harmed. What a heartache this is!

Now for the first time appears this new magazine 'The Spiritual Food Quarterly'. After months of preparation and prayer we send it forth, to be issued quarterly, and pray that God will watch over it. May it grow stronger and stronger, may it become more and more alive; may it serve those who need spiritual food. We ask, too, that it will help every reader to see more and more of God's glory, to experience more and more of His grace, to have a fuller understanding of His will, to obey Him more faithfully, to know His Son — our Lord Jesus Christ — more deeply, to watch and wait for His coming, and then to stand joyfully in His presence acceptable to Him. This is the prayer and hope of the editor"

Guiding principles

At the beginning it was our intention to publish only what God showed to me and also the messages that He had committed to me to transmit to others. In view of this we had no plans to seek manuscripts from others. But my friend Shih Tien-Min frequently translated helpful articles and from time to time we selected and printed some of them. I myself translated four books written by Mr G. H. Knight and these also appeared in the Quarterly. Two of these had already appeared separately, one being entitled 'In the secret place of fellowship'. The other was entitled 'In the dark and cloudy day'. Apart from this I have sometimes translated short passages and published them in the Quarterly. Otherwise, the majority of articles are what I myself have written.

During these more than twenty years I have followed a general pattern in the type of material used. Thus each issue has one section for a basic truth of the Bible and one section for some aspect of the Christian life. I also make a point of exposing apostate teaching and the work of false teachers. I also highlight and reprove the prevalent sins of the church and of the world. The articles I write correspond closely to what I preach. I do not like people to keep a record of what I preach, because there are very few who can record the messages accurately. There are often many discrepancies between what the preacher has preached and the records people have made. The errors are sometimes serious. In view of all this I feel that it is more important for me to write the manuscript.

In the early issues I used to put a comparatively long article right at the beginning. Then a Christian made a suggestion to me. 'When anyone reads the "Spiritual Food Quarterly" for the first time' he said, 'he may not have much time or he may not yet be really interested in the contents, and if he finds a long article right at the beginning he may quickly put it down and not be inclined to read it again. But if you put a short article at the beginning, the man with little interest will both be encouraged to read it.' What this brother said was logical and from then on I followed his suggestion.

Many readers have written over the years requesting that the quarterly be changed to a monthly. But I have never acceded to their request. The reason I decided on a quarterly in the first place was the fact of my strength being limited. And I have amply proved since then that I made the right decision. My literary work is only one of three spheres of responsibility. The others are the care of the church in Peking and my ministry away from Peking. Had we begun publishing a monthly the magazine would have folded up within one or two years.

Although the Spiritual Food Quarterly is administered by myself the finances are managed independently. Apart from the 200 dollars which I put into it at the beginning I have neither put money into it nor have I taken money out of it. Before the outbreak of war with Japan the sale of books and magazines produced an appropriate profit. Some of this was set aside to help towards the support of several preachers who look to the Lord for their support; the rest was used for printing more books. Thus over a period of 10 years we published more than 20 books. During the first year or two after the outbreak of war with Japan, since the change in commodity prices was only slight, we did not experience any appreciable difficulty. But then the value of the currency plunged calamitously and commodity prices rose like a flood, so our income gradually failed to catch up with our expenses. We raised the subscription price a little, but it was still inadequate. In the autumn of 1943 we changed type to economize in paper. But during the last three years of the war with Japan and the first three or four years afterwards prices soared so alarmingly that the increase in the subscription price was still far from adequate. One reason for this was our fear to add to the burden of subscribers and another reason was the fact that increases in subscription prices always lagged behind prices in general.

Some of the publications produced by China churches were subsidized by foreign missionary societies, so even when the number of subscribers dropped or when subscribers failed to send their subscriptions they still had no problem. But the Spiritual Food Quarterly received no support from foreign missionary societies and was not sponsored by any group or individual. The only capital it had had was the 200 dollars that I had contributed 23 years earlier. Were it not that God had constantly looked after me and given me wisdom to manage this publication I cannot imagine how we could have carried on publication for over 20 years.

I have filled several offices but I have never accepted a salary for any of those offices. Nor have I paid out any money in salaries. But my God has supplied all my need according to His riches in glory and I have lacked nothing. I have always been extremely busy but I have also been extremely happy. Each day I live I do one day's work. If God gets glory through the work I do, if people can derive benefit through the work I do, and if, in the future when I see the Lord, I can be described as His good and faithful servant, what reward can be possibly greater than that!

The fact is, when I write articles for the Quarterly I myself am invariably spiritually blessed. The more I write and pass on the teaching I receive from the Lord the more I receive comfort, encouragement and power from the Lord Himself. Further, when I have to write several articles without a break the Lord then gives me messages without a break. If someone had asked me 20 years ago to write more than 200,000 words I could not have imagined how I could write them. Yet after writing steadily for more than 20 years I have now completed that number. When I write words of reproof, I myself am reproved. When I write words of encouragement, I myself am encouraged. When I write words of comfort, I myself am comforted. When I help others, I myself am helped. These things are true both when I preach and when I write articles. No wonder the Lord Jesus said: 'Give, and it shall be given unto you; good measure, pressed down, and shaken together and running over, shall man give into bosom. For with the same measure that ye mete withal it shall measured to you again.'' (Luke 6: 38)

Apart from deriving spiritual benefit from writing articles I have also been able to make progress in my composition. There is a big difference between the phraseology of my writings 20 years ago and my writings today. And as a result of frequently consulting my dictionary I now write more accurately.

The writing of these articles has also helped me in my writing of doctrine. I have been warned by failures and mistakes in the past. Nowadays the doctrines which I really do not understand I do not preach; matters which I do not comprehend I do not proclaim; words and phrases that I really do not know I do not speak; quotations that are not clear to me I do not use. The words I speak, the phrases I use, the articles I write, the business I do, the paths I tread — I want all of these to be as perfect as possible. Naturally this is not something which can be achieved overnight. But that is my goal.

1st April 1950

7.
I will make a
helper suitable for
him...

Genesis 2:15 'The Lord God took the man and put him into the Garden of Eden to dress it and to keep it.'

Genesis 2:18 'The Lord God said, 'It is not good that the man should be alone. I will make him an help meet for him.'

God prepared a partner to help Adam whom He loved and whom He used. God makes a similar provision for others whom He also loves and uses. If they themselves are not hasty, if they do not depend on their own ideas, and if they humbly maintain an attitude of trusting and obeying God, if they allow God to guide them according to His good and acceptable will, they will surely find that the partner whom God provides is not only a good companion but also a good fellow-worker. Unfortunately many are in too much of a hurry and make a choice according to their own ideas and desires. At the time they consider that they have chosen an ideal partner but their own choice becomes a substitute for God's choice. As a result they not only forfeit the happiness and success that God wants to give them, they also bring upon themselves immeasurable grief and failure.

The choosing of a partner by Christian believers is a matter of the highest importance. In order to avoid failure we have no dependable method apart from looking to God with a single mind seeking His guidance. God has a plan for all who belong to Him. It is a perfect plan and one that brings His blessing. We must be careful that we do not destroy it. Alas, that is just what often happens. Some believers destroy it by being covetous; some by their love of vainglory; and others by failure to wait quietly for God's time. Some destroy God's plan through yielding to the desires of the flesh. So they suffer loss and bring upon themselves much suffering.

Some people feel that an ideal partner must be similar in disposition, but in my view this is not entirely true. The couples that God brings together are frequently different in temperament. It is true that this is sometimes a cause of friction, yet God can use this kind of friction to rub off rough corners and make them like smooth stones. (see 1 Samuel 17:40)

However, an ideal partner must hold the same beliefs and share the same purpose. If your partner is one with you in believing the Lord and in loving the Lord, you need not be concerned about perfect agreement in other matters. Least of all need you be swayed by riches, beauty and vainglory and thus lose an excellent partner whom God has provided for you. If a believer will wait quietly for the Lord then the Lord will provide a suitable partner — not necessarily one that he himself sees as good and suitable but one whom God sees as good and suitable.

A confirmed bachelor

There was a period in my life, between the ages of 21 and 24, when I desired to live as a bachelor. For one thing my circumstances were very difficult and my work was arduous; I had no hope whatever of a brighter path ahead. For another thing, when I considered the conditions then obtaining it seemed better not to marry. Also I had observed for a long time the friction in the courtyard between my mother and sister on the one hand and neighbours on the other and I was unwilling to set up a home where the same conditions of disorder and misery might be repeated. In addition to all this I had the impression at that time that unmarried believers were especially pure and spiritual. My mother observed this and she was very grieved. She had been a widow for more than 20 years and had only one son. It was her great hope that I would grow up and obtain employment, and that I would then take a wife and produce children. Seeing my leaning towards bachelorhood she feared that her hopes would vanish like bubbles. My mother was so concerned about this that she once delegated someone to come and urge me to abandon the thought of remaining unmarried. What of myself? In actual fact I nourished two ideas in conflict with each other. On the one hand I wished to remain unmarried but on the other hand I felt the need of a partner.

For a long time I could come to no conclusion one

way or the other. The matter of marriage was raised on two occasions during that period by brothers in the Lord. But in each case I made no response.

In the spring of 1925, when my work in Peking was growing, a lady who had known me for a long time frequently attended my meetings. She often came to talk to me and asked many questions. She also indicated that she wanted to be zealous in love for the Lord. I had the feeling, however, that her zeal was directed to me and not to the Lord. As a consequence I took care that we were not thrown together more than necessary. At one time she heard that I was going to travel and she said to me, 'Recently I have often heard you preaching and this has been a great help to me. Now that you are going away I shall be very lonely and I shall have nowhere to go to get help. While you are away can you still help me?' I realized that she really wanted me to correspond with her. But I realized that that would be unprofitable both for her and for me. So I replied: 'I can only pray for you; there is nothing else I can do.' I guessed correctly. When I returned from the south in the autumn someone was commissioned by members of her family to effect a formal introduction. I immediately declined the proposition. This brought an end to the matter, and she ceased to attend our meetings.

In May 1925 I went to visit several Christians in Nanking whom I had corresponded with for some time. While there I enquired of an elderly servant of God whether he had any opinion to express concerning the possibility of my being married. He acknowledged that remaining single had advantages and being married had advantages. On the whole there was nothing against an older preacher being unmarried but when a young preacher remained unmarried he could not avoid many difficulties and inconveniences. I turned this over in my mind and accepted that what he said was logical. So I gave up the thought of remaining single.

My stay in Nanking lasted 14 days. Before going to Nanking I had had no thought of visiting Hangjou. I had heard even from my childhood of the beautiful scenery at the West Lake at Hangjou and it occurred to me that it was an opportune time to make a trip there. A sister in the Lord in Nanking, on hearing that I wished to visit Hangjou, gave me an introduction to her aunt. Another sister introduced me to a brother in the Lord with whom she was acquainted. So when I reached Hangjou on June 16th I called on that brother and asked him to recommend a suitable hotel. He pressed me to stay in his home, but because the sister in Nanking had given me an introduction to her aunt I felt that I should visit her first. So on June 22nd I paid my respects to an elderly lady, Mrs Li at Tien-Shui Bridge. She in turn introduced me to the pastor of the church there — Pastor Liu Deh-Shun — and his wife.

Mr Liu called on me on June 26th and invited me to preach at his church. I agreed to do this and preached both morning and afternoon on the following Sunday. The believers there then invited me to lead a series of meetings for them, and again I agreed. However the place where I was staying was a considerable distance from Tien-Shui Bridge so Mr Liu urged me to stay with him. So on the 30th I moved over to his home.

On July 3rd I left Hangjo and went to Jia-Hsing, where I led meetings for 10 days, and then I took the train for Shanghai. I intended to get a boat from Shanghai to Fujo (the capital of the Province of Fujien) but while I was awaiting a passage I suddenly became ill. Not only was there no one in the hotel to look after me, but the other visitors in the hotel played cards throughout the night and it was impossible to sleep even a little. Knowing no one really well in Shanghai I had no alternative but to hurry home. But the journey would take two or three days, and at Nanking I should need to change trains and cross the river. To make such a journey and in my condition seemed impossible. In the midst of these multiplied troubles I suddenly thought of Pastor and Mrs Liu at Hangjo who had treated me so kindly and compassionately. The journey from Shanghai to Hangjo took only 4 or 5 hours, so I decided to return to Hangjo immediately. I thus returned on the 17th. Resting for several days in Hangjo I gradually recovered from my illness. I then accepted an invitation to lead another series of meetings lasting 12 days at the church in Chieng-Tien-Shui Bridge. I also visited other places in the area and did not leave for Peking until September 9th.

I arrived back in Peking on September 14th. Soon after I received an express letter from Mr Liu in Hangjo. He announced that the churches of Hangjo were to hold meetings over a period of seven days in October, and because some of the believers in Hangjo had been helped by my earlier ministry they invited me to be the speaker. After praying about it for two days I sent a letter accepting the invitation.

Since the meetings were scheduled to begin on October 18th I planned to leave Peking on 15th. But unexpectedly the two provinces Jiangsu (where Shanghai is situated) and Jejiang (where Hangjo is situated) became the scene of fierce fighting and all the railways were cut. I then heard that it was possible to travel by steamship from Tienjin to Shanghai, and since the fighting had already spread to the railway between those two cities I decided to travel by sea. I left Tienjin on 27th, and since the railway south from Shanghai had been re-opened I reached Hangjo in time to begin my delayed ministry on November 4th. The meetings lasted a week. Those responsible for the meetings knew that I was already acquainted with Pastor and Mrs Liu and they had arranged for them to entertain me. Thus I stayed with them for the third time.

Meets future wife

On the second day of the convention the lady who normally played the organ had an engagement and could not attend. So they asked Mr Liu's daughter, Miss Liu Jing-Wun, to take her place. Although I had been acquainted with Miss Liu for more than 20 days, I had heard that she was 16 or 17 years old and I had not taken particular notice of her, since I looked upon her as a child. Up to that time it had been my impression that only men and women whose ages were approximately the same could be married to each other — allowing a difference of one or two years at the most. Since there was a difference of 8 or 9 years between my age and that of Miss Liu it had never occurred to me to think of the possibility of our being married. But when I saw her playing the organ I suddenly realized that she was not just a child in her early teens. She was tall; she had a mature hair-style; she was wearing a long lined gown; she was

indeed an adult (in fact she was at that time a school-teacher). Although she had been a student for 10 years in a Girls' School run by the Episcopal Church, and all along had attended services at the episcopal Hsin-I Church (where presumably the convention was being held) she had never before played the organ there. It was in fact the first and last time. But as she played the organ on that one occasion I realized for the first time that she was an adult.

On the three occasions that I stayed in the home of Mr and Mrs Liu I was greatly favoured by their concern and love; I had already been conscious of the spiritual warmth in the home. I had never known my father. My mother greatly loved me, and relations with my mother and sister were good; but in the home we did not breathe a spiritual atmosphere. Feelings were strained between my mother and sister on the one hand and my aunt on the other. And between them and the neighbours who lived in the same courtyard there was constant bickering. Indeed what I saw and heard at home always made me very unhappy. We had no peace, no joy, no harmony, and no consideration. All that my mother knew was love for her children. All that my sister knew was love for her mother and younger brother. My mother and sister felt that there was no basis for loving outsiders. After I believed in the Lord this attitude gave me great pain and sorrow. So when I stayed in the home of Mr and Mrs Liu I was especially conscious of the harmony and joy which pervaded it. So from the day that I discovered that Miss Liu was not a child but an adult I began to wonder whether the partner whom God was preparing for me was not in fact right there.

I remained in the area taking meetings for another 20 days and during that time I turned the matter over and over in my mind and prayed about it earnestly. I was fearful of taking a wrong step which would bring a lifetime of sorrow and failure. On November 29th I prayed about it specially and in the evening I talked the matter over with an elderly sister. I asked for her opinion and sought her guidance. She promised to pray about it and then to see if there was anything she could do. I learned after a few days that Mr and Mrs Liu had neither assented to my proposition nor refused it. They recognized that the matter needed careful consideration. And what about Miss Jing-Wun herself? When her mother asked what she felt she replied: 'What my heavenly Father sees is good, that is good.'

From the end of November 1925 until the end of April 1926 I was engaged in ministry in the two provinces Jiangsu and Jejiang and during periods of rest I returned to Hangjo. In discussing marriage neither of us came to any decision; we only waited for God to reveal His will to us. At the same time it was possible for us to become more closely acquainted with each other.

But I still had to remain in ignorance of the thinking of my mother and sister, for I feared that informing them by letter might create misunderstanding and I decided to discuss the matter in person when I returned to Peking. On several occasions in the past my mother had said that if I ever planned to get married I must marry a woman from Peking, and more than that she must be someone known to her. My mother had a prejudice and considered that people from anywhere outside Peking were inferior. As for southerners they were even worse. From time to time we had had families from the south living in our courtyard and my mother always referred to them as 'southern barbarians'. So it was highly probable that the proposed marriage with Miss Liu would encounter opposition from my mother. But if this thing were of God I believed that He could change my mother's heart, and make her approve. If God Himself disapproved then I trusted Him to hinder us through my mother's opposition. From before my birth my mother had lived in widowhood, and for more than 20 years she had worked very hard for me, bringing me up to manhood. I had to be filial to her and obey her. I decided that I would not wound my mother over my marriage. So if my mother indicated disapproval I would drop the matter and go no further with it. Mr and Mrs Liu approved of my decision and constantly urged me to respect my mother.

On May 10th 1926 I returned to my home in Peking and two days later I talked with my mother and sister concerning my projected marriage to Miss Liu. They uttered no word of disapproval. Moreover they considered that there could not possibly be anything wrong with my way of looking at it. The final evidence that I sought from God had now been given. I now knew that for us to be married was the good, acceptable, and perfect will of God.

Engagement and marriage

I stayed at home for 21 days and on June 1st I again took a boat for the south to minister in Shao-Hsing in Jejiang. Afterwards I preached successively at various other places in the area. On November 24th in Hangjo I was engaged to Jing-Wun. After ministering elsewhere in the south I returned to Peking at the end of December. After that I again visited Manchuria.

From the time of my departure from Hangjo I did

not go south again for seventeen months. And not until June 1928 did I return to Hangjo. On August 8th, at a quarter past eleven in the morning, I was married in Hangjo to Miss Liu Jing-Wun. The service was conducted by the elderly Pastor Run Jih-Ching of the China Inland Mission. Pastor Run had been the teacher of my father-in-law, a devout and loveable elderly gentleman. He read Genesis Chapter 2 and Chapter 24, and he based his message on two couples — Adam and Eve, and Isaac and Rebecca. He spoke at some length and in the hot weather I was perspiring profusely. Nevertheless I received much teaching and encouragement.

Although my wife and I had known each other for over a year before our engagement, at no time had we been on terms of friendship in the manner of young men and women today. On several occasions she raised certain questions about doctrine, but apart from this we never had any talks by ourselves, and normally when we talked with one another it was together with her parents. Only after we were engaged in the winter of 1926, when I returned to the north, did we begin to correspond. Someone enquired whether our marriage was new style or old style. I could only reply: 'Neither new nor old; both new and old; half new half old.'

At the time of our wedding an elderly sister in the Lord lent us her house while she was away 'escaping the heat'. The chapel and the buildings of the Women's Bible School were in the centre; Mr Liu's house was on the east side and the house on loan to us was on the west side. So on the wedding day we did not need any vehicles. Leaving the chapel we passed the gates of two courtyards and we then came to the house we were using.

My mother-in-law gave each of us a Bible on the wedding day. In mine she had written: 'Take heed unto thyself, and unto the doctrine; continue in them: for in doing this thou shalt both save thyself, and them that hear thee.' (1 Timothy 4:16). In my wife's was: 'Don't let anyone look down on you because you are young, but set an example for the believers in speech, in life, in love, in faith and in purity.' (1 Timothy 4:12).

I was born on July 25th, 1900, and my wife was born on March 29th, 1909. I am thus 8 years 8 months and 4 days older than she is. On the day of our wedding I had just passed my 28th birthday and my wife was not yet 20. From the time we began to discuss the possibility of our marrying to our engagement was one year, and from our engagement to our wedding day was 1 year and 8 months. My friend Shih Tien-min presented us with a pair of scrolls . . .

God's providence

My wife and I, looking back, could see the amazing way in which God had led us. On the occasion of my first visit to Hangjo, if I had not gone to pay my respects to Miss Liu I would never have got to know Mr and Mrs Liu. And on returning to Shanghai from Jejiang, if I had not become ill at Shanghai I would never have returned to the home of Mr Liu in Hangjo. Both the first visit and the later illness were plainly by the will of God. It was also a very wonderful thing that my mother and my sister agreed to the marriage. And when you think of their attitude to us after the marriage had taken place (as will be described later) their agreement was all the more wonderful. I truly believe that their assent at the time was of God. Their dissatisfaction later was also of God, so that through a period of testing both of us might learn the lessons that we ought to learn. Although I am from Peking, God most wonderfully led me south of the River Yangtze so that I might meet the one whom He had provided as a partner for me. How marvellous are His works!

Before my wife and I were engaged my mother-in-law-to-be had heard of the various ways in which God had disciplined me. She one day posed the question: 'Is it necessary for everyone whom God wants to use to experience discipline? I replied: 'I think it is that way.' She said, 'Then what about a girl like Jing-Wun who has never experienced discipline like this?' At the time I was unable to say anything. Nor did I stop to think whether she had really experienced discipline. But after we were married it was not long before discipline came to her.

We left Hangjo on August 31st and on September 9th we took a boat from Shanghai for Ching-Dao. After a ministry lasting several weeks in Ching-Dao we then went on by boat to Tienjin, arriving at Peking on 18th.

A strange reaction

As soon as we reached home we encountered a trial that was totally unexpected. Whenever I had returned home on previous occasions, if my mother and my sister knew the day, they would prepare most appetizing food in good time to await my return. On the day of our return as man and wife we arrived at 4 o'clock in the afternoon. We found my mother and sister most strangely cool. At 5 o'clock my wife and I went to the station to collect our baggage and we had to wait some time before we could get it. When we eventually got home at half past six my mother said to me, "We, (meaning herself, my sister and the girl helper,) have already eaten. You two go ahead and prepare food for yourselves." All that we could do was to go on the street and buy some food. Then my wife and I ate it together. Confronted with a situation of this nature my heart was like ice. I had anticipated that when my mother and my sister saw my wife and me together they would be extremely happy and that we should enjoy each other's company. Who could imagine that we should be treated like this?

The next morning in the inner courtyard my sister began to raise her voice and make a disturbance. I knew that it was directed against my wife and me. But I failed to understand the reason for it. I began to weep in my room and my wife also wept tears of sympathy. I could not understand what lay behind it; my wife understood even less. We could not, for the Lord's sake, give vent to our feelings. We could only endure it.

From that time on our home was full of suspicion, hate, bad feeling, quarrelling and restlessness. I kept my eyes and ears open and I gradually understood the origin of the trouble. It arose mainly from prejudice and misunderstanding on the part of my mother and sister. But I also contributed to it by lack of experience and commonsense.

I recalled an occasion during my teens when my mother remarked to my sister and me, 'If you have any matter on your minds let us talk about it now. In the future, when you, Yong-shung, are married, there will be a stranger in the home and we shall no longer be able to discuss intimate matters.' At the time I had no inkling of what lay behind these words. But although they were spoken more than ten years before my marriage they revealed the fact that in the eyes of my mother a daughter-in-law was an outsider. They also showed my mother's pattern of thought, that 'when the son is married he will inevitably change his attitudes; no longer will he love his mother and sister and no longer will he be of one heart with them.' This outlook was strongly established and no matter how filial the son and daughter-in-law were, it would be extremely difficult for them to win acceptance.

Bitter experience

I did not blame my mother and sister for taking this position. They had been greatly influenced by the things that they had experienced and by the circumstances in which they had been placed. Living with the three of us in the same courtyard there had been my grandmother and my aunt. My aunt was three years younger than my mother and she had never been married. My mother was simple and honest whereas my aunt was clever and scheming. Although living in the same home each looked after her own affairs and ate her own food. At first my mother had greatly loved her younger sister, remembering that while she (my mother) had two surviving children my aunt was unmarried. My mother constantly took gifts to her sister. But when my aunt saw that my mother was honest and generous she constantly devised means of getting hold of mother's belongings. But when my mother had needs and sought help from my aunt, my aunt refused to give her anything at all. So although my mother's things were continually used by my aunt, my aunt's things were not only unavailable for my mother to use but closely hidden away. If ever my aunt wished to use my mother's things she simply came and took them. For a while my mother let this go on but eventually she was forced to take notice of it. The fact is, my mother's possessions were growing fewer and fewer and she could no longer afford to be generous. But when my aunt observed that she could not continue to get things from my mother her attitude changed and she became cold and cruel. This made my mother suffer acutely. So although originally my mother had loved her younger sister with all her heart, they now reached the state of continually clashing. My mother was sharply provoked. If her own sister was like this, where in all the world could she find someone who could be relied on not to seek to injure or harm her? It marked a turning-point. From that time on my mother would not trust anyone.

Nor could she find anyone of integrity among all the neighbours who shared the courtyard with her. What she saw there was a scenario of unfilial children, daughters-in-law who were harsh to their mothers-in-law, husbands who oppressed their wives, wives who insulted their husbands, step-mothers who ill-treated the children of a former wife, and brothers who hated each other and often fought each other. She lived with neighbours who told lies and who were constantly embroiled in quarrelling; these were everyday occurrences.

Think of my mother's situation — with 10 families crowded into a small courtyard. There were constant changes with people moving in and people moving out. My mother was an ordinary widow with two small children, and their life was unavoidably bound up with people like this. She was in a cruel dilemma. She had no means of supporting herself and unless she rented out the rooms she had no income. But as a result of renting out the rooms my mother would be taken advantage of and she would get angry and give way to tears. It was 20 years of bitter experience that forced her to the conclusion that nowhere in the world could she find anyone to be relied on as genuinely good.

My mother judged the world at large by the neighbours with whom she shared a courtyard. She came to the conclusion that no child anywhere was filial, that every daughter-in-law treated her mother-in-law harshly, that in all married couples the stronger oppressed the weaker, that all brothers and sisters hated each other and treated each other cruelly and that the predominant purpose of all social intercourse was to use each other, to deceive each other, to harm each other and to oppress each other. Although my mother had been baptized as an infant and later joined the church, she had only rarely seen people who were sincere and honest and who truly loved the Lord. What she saw, even there, was lying, vanity, envy, strife, covetousness, depravity, and self-seeking. Unbelieving neighbours were like that; so-called Christians were also like that. Thus my mother came to the conclusion that no matter whether people were believers or unbelievers not one among them was upright and trustworthy.

My sister was knowledgeable and in character she was honest, but in disposition she was headstrong and proud. My sister and I were both well placed at school and our mother praised us because we won prizes. But unconsciously this made both of us proud and conceited. We tended to look down on those less gifted. This led inevitably to friction and conflict. Add to this the fact that our mother spoiled us and this made us people who were most difficult to deal with. Fortunately I was saved when I was 14 years old and my life was completely transformed. My sister, however, did not experience a change of this nature. I talked to her about the Gospel and at that time she was moved to tears and willing to receive it. But in 1921 she worked for a year among young people in a certain church in Peking, and the conduct of the person in charge of that church, who had neither faith nor morals, was so depraved that my sister often told people that 'All preachers say one thing and mean another; they are hypocrites; they only do the work of preaching as a means of livelihood. My brother is a simpleton.' Since my sister felt like this she could neither give credence to anyone nor could she love anyone. She was a student for about ten years and she spent about ten years as a teacher. But never in all that time did she have a regular friend. As a result of this she became more and more aloof. She was naturally clever and her intuition was extremely accurate. This made her more and more self-confident and at the same time encouraged her to grow suspicious of people. Because she came to think herself incapable of error, when she formed the judgement that a certain person was wicked, nothing would make her change her attitude, no matter what evidence you adduced to the contrary.

Neither my mother nor my sister was basically wicked. They would neither revile anyone nor strike anyone. Yet when mother and daughter were together for any length of time they frequently became suspicious that a particular person was harbouring evil, or hatching a wicked plot, or scheming to harm them, or planning to rob them of their gains. Here again I find it difficult to blame them. For 20 years they had been repeatedly deceived and they had had 'to eat a great deal of bitterness.'

A sore trial

With all this in the background there came into their lives a young woman whom they had not hitherto known. As a result of their experiences over the years they invested this intruder with an image resulting from all their suspicions. It so happened that this young woman had grown up in an extremely simple and wholesome environment. She never dreamed that she would be the object of appraisal and suspicion. She was too young to have experienced the ramification of society in general and because she came from south of the river she was ignorant of the customs, habits, feelings, and manners of the north. You must add to this the fact that she could not speak Pekingese. For all these things she became the object of censure.

It is said that a man is normally broad-minded and a woman narrow-minded. In the case of my wife and myself the reverse is true. Because of this my heart was pierced more deeply than my wife's. There were matters of conjecture that my sister regarded as facts, and she talked about these to my mother. Since my mother knew that my sister was clever she accepted the views of my sister without question. Then came confusion — layer upon layer without end. Although my mother misunderstood us, because she loved her son she kept herself under control. My sister, however, often lost her temper, and at times she would shout and rave. In the evening we often overheard my sister giving vent to angry harangues until 2 or 3 o'clock in the morning. My wife was unwilling to listen to this shouting or to take any notice of it, but it brought her much suffering, and sometimes upset her. I for my part listened to it, but this only added to my pain and sorrow.

From the time that my wife came to our home I became, in the eyes of my mother and my sister, an outsider. They would often not speak to me. It was not that they had ceased to love me, but it was due to their assumption that my heart was no longer directed towards them. In fact, of course, my love for them had not in any way grown less because I now had a wife. God is my witness that if at any time I had food that was specially palatable I would first think of my mother. Whenever I was invited to a feast I thought of my mother being unable to participate and I would buy some especially tasty food and take it home to her. I stated on one occasion that I would rather sacrifice my wife than sacrifice my mother. But I realized afterwards that this was wrong. For while I had only one mother I also had only one wife. A son ought to love his mother; but a husband also ought to love his wife. You can neither abandon a mother for a wife nor abandon a wife for a mother. I bent every effort to sympathize with and comfort my mother; I also did the same for my wife. In spite of this my mother still regarded me as an outsider, considering that my heart now belonged to my wife.

My mother acknowledged that I still treated her very well. But she could not trust me. 'Having taken a wife he no longer needs his mother' is the saying. Prejudice of this kind made my mother erect a high wall between her and me. It was as solid as concrete. At the beginning it was only my sister who could remove this high wall, because she and my mother were on speaking terms. Previously, whenever my mother quarrelled with our neighbours, I did all I could to make peace, explaining that not all the blame should be placed on the neighbours and that in some ways we ourselves were at fault. My sister, however, invariably aided my mother by expatiating on the faults and shortcomings of the neighbours. My own hope was to throw a bowl of water over the flames of my mother's anger, but what my sister took was a jar of oil. I was prompted in what I did by love for my mother, but my mother considered that I leaned towards the neighbours and that I was thus inflicting injury on my own family. Under these circumstances my mother was pleased with my sister and accepted what she said. Had my sister only assured my mother that my heart was unchanged my mother's prejudice would have been dissolved. Alas! My sister also took the view that I was sheltering outsiders. Since my mother and my sister were of one mind in this the wall between us not only resisted all our efforts to break it down, it became even bigger and stronger.

Naturally if I had simply hardened my heart the situation would have been easier to handle. Irrespective of any sorrow that might be occasioned for my mother and sister I could have adopted the attidue that it did not concern us. I should have been spared a great deal of suffering. But as it was I loved my mother and my sister. Yet they persisted in regarding me as an outsider and rejecting my love. I myself was wounded and I was troubled for my mother and sister. I could not bear to see my white-haired old mother and the sister born from the same womb continue to live a life of such bitterness. It was a tragic situation.

I urge all who are parents on no account to harbour this kind of prejudice — regarding it as axiomatic that a son who takes a wife will cease to love his parents. I recognize that there are some sons who do act in this way and cease to love their parents; but their numbers are few. For parents to harbour such a prejudice brings sorrow both to themselves and to their off-spring. And sons who do not love their parents fully may be forced to part company altogether. Parents should realize that to be misunderstood and to be unjustly condemned is an extremely painful experience.

Wise parents, after the marriage of their sons, should not only treat their sons well but should also treat their daughters-in-law well.

Deep feelings

The main reason for this friction in our home was the depth of prejudice. Another reason was my own lack of experience. Before the matter of my proposed marriage had been raised I had repeatedly used the Word of the Lord to exhort my sister both face to face and in correspondence. Sometimes I spoke forthrightly and severely. Because my sister loved me, even when she did not receive my exhortation she did not reprove me. After I became engaged, not knowing that my sister had a prejudice towards me, I treated her in exactly the same way as before. And once or twice, when I was away from home, I wrote letters exhorting her in which my words were both earnest and severe. My heart was unchanged; my exhortation was unchanged. Who would imagine that on account of these letters my sister would become angry? She complained that if I condemned her sin and attacked her in that way before I was married, what kind of ill-treatment might she not expect after my marriage.

Several months before my marriage (that is, during the engagement period) the girl whom we employed used a rope to thread fish. She was a little careless and dropped the rope in a tub of dirty water. My sister observed it and immediately reprimanded her. The servant girl quickly snatched it out and washed it in clean water. She was about to thread the fish on it but my sister stopped her, saying that since the rope had already been in dirty water it could not be used. The girl then looked for another rope, but my sister still objected, saying that she must use the original rope. So the servant girl again used clean water to wash the original rope. But my sister still made a fuss. 'I have washed it' said the girl, 'and you say it is still unclean. I get another rope and you say it is still no good. I wash the original rope again and you still say it is unclean. What do you really want me to do?' Then my sister said, 'I want the original rope before it fell into the dirty water. No other rope will do.' As an onlooker I couln't let this pass. So I found another rope and gave it to the girl saying, 'Here is a clean one; use this!' But my sister was still not satisfied. 'No other rope will do,' she said to the girl, 'You must use the original rope before it fell into the dirty water.' I saw that my sister was treating the girl harshly and I said to her, 'She also is a person; why are you bothering her in this way? How can she possibly use the rope before it fell into the water? You can take her life but she still can't do it.' It was no good. What I said only aroused her more. She jumped into the air and shouted to me, 'Your wife has still not entered the door (that is, you are still not married) and you treat your sister like this. You are helping the servant and oppressing your sister. What will you do to me in the future when you are married?'

If my recollection is not faulty my sister had never rowed with me like that since the time I was ten. We had lived in the same house with particular harmony. If at any time before my engagement I had used the same words as I used on this particular day they could not have provoked such an incident. But because on that occasion I had already been engaged for a year and a half my sister, who had already become prejudiced, considered that I had already changed my attitude and that I wanted to vex her. Since I was a younger brother I could not quarrel with my sister; I therefore made no further reply and withdrew to my room. My sister was in a thoroughly bad temper and for half a day she would not speak to me. When it was time for the evening meal I went and invited my sister to come and eat. She wept and I wept.

I had no idea that my mother and my sister had developed a prejudice against me from the time of my engagement. Many of the things I said to them during that period in all innocence were construed by them as carrying an ulterior motive. Doubt and suspicion arose and as time went on the situation worsened. However, since in reality my sister loved me, she did not allow the situation to develop too far. So that is how it continued right until the coming of my wife. And then my sister cast off all restraint, apparently caring nothing about me whatever. At bottom, my mother still had a particular love for her son, and often when my sister was in a particular turbulent mood my mother feared that it would grieve me and sought to restrain her. But my sister then charged that my mother was sheltering us and quarrelled with her. For me to live in circumstances like this meant anguish.

Grace given

Thank God! In the midst of adversity we have experienced God's grace in abundance. Although my wife encountered all these trials in the home she never at any time uttered complaint. Her attitude was based on the conviction that she had been brought into this situation not by man but by God. Moreover she constantly encouraged me and comforted me. She was still not 20 years old. She had accompanied her husband to a place 3,000 miles from her own home and apart from her husband she did not possess a single acquaintance in Peking. And after all that she encountered the buffetting of waves like this. In the nature of the case she would be involved in suffering far greater than mine. But she met all these trials with a tranquil temperament and in this way she took the edge off my own suffering. Just suppose my wife had added her own grumbles and complaints to the treatment meted out by my mother and my sister, how vastly greater would have been my own grief and sorrow. But far from complaining she only gave comfort and encouragement.

The days that my wife and I passed through for a very long time were extremely frightening. We could never tell when my sister would suddenly lose her temper. We were always alert; we dare not talk to her much; but even so we never knew what word of ours would create misunderstanding. Sometimes we would return home from outside and as soon as we entered the side road leading to our house we became tense. Every time I returned from ministry elsewhere, after emerging from the railway station and engaging a rickshaw, my heart would begin to palpitate. I was restless, for I could not tell what tone of voice or what kind of expression awaited me in the home. My wife and I suffered; my sister also suffered.

Whatever wrongs my wife suffered at home during my absences for ministry she never talked of her grievances when I returned. Sometimes I listened to the unreasonable talk of my sister and my heart found it impossible to bear. But my wife would say to me: 'We must not blame elder sister. It is not that she clearly knows I have no fault and that she purposely causes me grief. In her eyes I am really bad, so it is not surprising that she is dissatisfied with me. If I were in her place I also would be capable of losing my temper. There are few people in the world who would oppress others without any cause whatever.' As soon as she said this I relaxed and the anger in my heart melted. Sometimes she would hear my sister in a bout of temper, and in the outer courtyard she would quietly sing hymns so that she would not have to listen to unseemly expressions and thus be able to avoid provocation. She had never contradicted my sister, explaining her attitude in this way: 'If I clash with my sister, how can I continue living with her? Since we must all pass our days together, we do not want on account of passing unhappiness to mar our friendly relations.'

(Strangely I have not seen any account of the birth of their son. But the presence in the home of their child is now assumed).

We also have cause to thank God in that our son of only a few years, in the midst of grandmother, aunt and parents, has never passed on any talk from one to the other. Whatever he heard when with his aunt or grandmother he never mentioned it to us. Nor did he mention the conversation of his parents when he was with his aunt or grandmother. Naturally we never questioned him. Sometimes his aunt would enquire about our affairs but he would talk about something else. If his aunt persisted in questioning him he would smilingly reply, 'It doesn't concern me; it doesn't concern me!' It was God's grace in the midst of our trials that the child in the home never stirred up any trouble.

When my wife first encountered all these troubles she naturally felt ill at ease and shed many tears. But from beginning to end she was fully persuaded that none of these troubles came upon her without the permission of a compassionate Father God. Since her suffering was only by the permission of God she realized that He had lessons He wanted to teach her. So she subdued her own feelings and did not allow herself to lose her temper. After an extended period of testing she not only had a fuller understanding of herself but also a deeper knowledge of the heart of God.

Severe testing

Of all the trials that we endured in our home the most serious were on two occasions which I will now describe.

In the spring of 1931 my wife became ill with a persistent cough and she was left without any strength. She went to hospital for an examination and it was discovered that the apex of both lungs showed signs of tubercles. The condition became worse every day. I was constantly absent from home engaged in ministry and not only did my wife have a child under two to look after but also the situation at home was most unhappy. The doctor urged my wife to have a change and to take a rest for a while. But my mother and my sister considered that she was only looking for an excuse to leave home. On April 10th I accompanied my wife to the hospital for another examination. The doctor said that it was certainly tuberculosis and that she would need to have a rest at least for several months. He added that if the trouble was not soon cleared up it could possibly be fatal. He further enquired whether I could take her to a sanatorium.

I returned home and explained to my mother and my sister the result of the examination. They took the view that my wife was not really suffering from tuberculosis but that she merely wanted to go away. My sister even became angry with me. She said that they had not been to the hospital and they questioned the result of the examination. I pressed them to go to the hospital to enquire of the doctor, but they replied that they had no time to go. At that time I was so worked up I cannot describe it. After a few days I again accompanied my wife to the German hospital and an X-ray was taken. I took this home to let my mother and my sister see it. They then objected that they did not understand it, as if my wife and I had conspired to deceive them. 'All who know me,' I said, 'believe what I say to them. On no account do they doubt me; on no account do they persist in asking whether it is true.'

Before my marriage my mother and my sister had always believed me, but since then they have continually doubted what I say. This brought indescribable grief. Now that my wife was so ill it was an even greater grief to me that they should insist that there was nothing wrong with her and object to her going to a sanatorium. If I took her away against their wishes it would arouse such a storm as would not bear thinking of.

In the middle of May, when I was leading meetings at Hwong-Hsien, the church there invited me to come again in the summer. I explained that because my wife was ill at home I could not accept their invitation. As soon as they heard of my wife's illness and her need of rest they invited me to take her to Hwong-Hsien and stay for a while. One of the sisters in the church expressed her willingness to look after her. On June 6th I returned to Peking and after much parleying — and only then — I was able to take my wife away. She stayed in Hwong-Hsien for four months.

At the beginning of November she travelled south with me from the province of Shan-Dong and returned to her parents' home in Hangjo. She stayed there for over a year and after this long period of rest her condition improved. Then in December 1932 she came back with me to Peking.

Two and a half years later, in the summer of 1934, my father-in-law became ill with cancer of the stomach. His condition was very grave and he was taken from Hangjo to Shanghai for surgery. My wife's brother, fearing the condition was dangerous, wrote and told us about it in the hope that my wife could pay her father a visit. When I showed the letter to my mother and sister my sister cried angrily, 'I also would like to make a trip to Shanghai and Hangjo.' The implication was that my father-in-law was not really ill and that the purpose of my brother-in-law's letter was to facilitate my wife going down there for a while on a holiday trip. Talk of that nature in the circumstances then obtaining was almost impossible to bear. I replied: 'Her father's illness is dangerous; naturally the daughter must visit him.' We had words over this and then my sister began to jump around while shouting, 'I will take a sword and kill someone.' Naturally my sister neither could nor would kill anyone. But when she lost her temper she gave utterance to all kinds of frightening expressions.

I was greatly vexed and disturbed. My father-in-law's illness was very serious and if my wife could not visit him I would be offending my father-in-law. But if, on the other hand, I sent my wife away irrespective of the feelings of my mother and sister, it could only give rise to a big disturbance. I became so worried I wanted to kill myself. I realize that apart from my own testimony you would never believe this; but it is an indication of my anxiety and anguish. My brother-in-law then wrote to say that my father-in-law's coffin had already been sent from Hangjou to Shanghai (in accordance with Chinese custom) and he feared that unless my wife could go soon then father and daughter would not meet, and this would be a matter for regret for the rest of her life. I showed this letter to my mother who feared that I was in a state in which I could worry myself into some catastrophe and she gave permission for us to go. Ten days later we left for the south. Shortly before we left my sister again became peevish and went out on purpose not to meet us. But after we reached Shanghai I received a letter from my sister who said that she had seen me and my wife in rickshaws on the way to the station. She had thought of calling to us but could not bring herself to do so. After we had gone she feared that she had caused us sorrow and had grieved over it; she acknowledged that to treat us in that way was to give us cause to be offended. My sister never ceased to love me but because she couldn't rid herself of this suspicious attitude towards my wife she continued to be resentful and restless. It was only when she heard of the death of my father-in-law that she really accepted the fact that we were not deceiving her. After we returned home she made no gesture of any kind but her attitude towards my wife greatly improved.

We did not hate my sister in the slightest; nor did we blame her. We considered that this was a kind of illness — an illness making people suspicious. It is right to overlook the actions of people who are ill, no matter how they give offence. We regarded my sister as sick. The illness which made her suspicious of people brought her bitterness and many years of suffering. If anyone who reads this is inclined to be suspicious of people I urge you to turn from it and to take it, as a serious illness that can do you much harm, into the presence of the Lord and ask Him to heal you. Otherwise you suffer yourself and you cause others to suffer.

8.
Learning from each other...

Twelve years after my wife and I had been married there arose friction between us because in several ways our temperaments were different from each other. I for my part like everything to be neat and tidy whereas she is inclined to be careless. For instance, before I was married I could manage all right at night without a lamp since I had a settled place for everything and I could readily lay hands on anything I wanted. She on her part would put things down according to the impulse of the moment, and if she wanted anything even in daylight she would have to spend a long time looking for it. Even if I arranged a room neatly and tidily in the morning everything would be scattered around before noon. It is not that she doesn't like a room to be tidy but the process of tidying up has to wait until she is ready to work on it. She then goes at it hard. But the room would soon be untidy again. I on my part prefer to tidy up as the need arises so that both rooms and courtyards are clean and tidy from morning until evening. Whenever I see a room untidy I fret over it. Sometimes I set to and tidy it; at other times I get angry and make a fuss. She never changed her habit and that made me even angrier.

In another respect our dispositions are entirely different. I am very careful even in regard to details and am unwilling to overlook any kind of error. But my wife is only conerned about the general effect. Whenever I write a letter I always read it through at least once before I post it. If the letter is important I read it through two or three times. But when my wife writes a letter she doesn't bother to read it through even once. This means that her letters are often sent off with omissions and words written incorrectly. Before our marriage, when she was still in Hangjo, there was one occasion when she finished writing a letter, put it in the envelope, sealed it, and stuck on the stamp. She then posted it with another letter. But she had omitted to write anything on the envelope. The pillar box happened to be near her home and because her family often posted letters there the postman took it to the home enquiring whether it was theirs. Only then did she become aware that she had omitted to write the address.

On one occasion after we were married an express letter arrived asking me to preach, and an envelope was enclosed with enough money for the reply to be sent by express. I was requested to answer as soon as possible. At the time I happened to be ministering in another province and my wife, having noted the purport of the letter, put it on one side. She neither replied to it nor forwarded it to me. I discovered the letter on my return, when it was already two months after the time fixed for the meetings. I could only write a letter of explanation and apology.

On another occasion when I was working in another province I received a letter from my wife who mentioned that three days previously she had forwarded three letters to me. But not one of them had I received. When I returned home I asked her whether she had in fact forwarded them to me and she said that she clearly remembered writing the forwarding address on the three envelopes. We concluded that they must have been lost in the post. However, after a number of days, I discovered the three letters behind the sewing machine. I frequently get angry and excited over things like this, but what does this achieve? It not only fails to repair the damage it also creates unrest. I gradually ceased to give way to anger on this account.

On another occasion the following amusing event occurred. My wife was hurrying to attend a meeting and she took the opportunity to take an old pair of leather shoes to the boot repairer. Being in a hurry she just put the paper bag on the counter and turned to leave. The boot repairer wanted her to open the bag and show what kind of repair she needed. But she explained: 'I'm in a hurry and have to go. You have a look and repair them where they are worn. That'll be O.K.' However she had only gone a few steps when the bootmaker called her back. For when he had opened the wrapping he discovered that the contents were not shoes but three salted pig trotters. They had

been sent by her mother from Hangjo. To me it was unbelievable, but it was all due to her happy-go-lucky disposition. Since I for my part am always particularly careful it was a case of God using a wife like this to rub me like a stone and make me smooth. Amazing!

My wife was not only happy-go-lucky she was also very forgetful. Sometimes she would promise to go and talk to someone at a certain place at a certain time. But when it came to the time of her visit the whole arrangement had gone completely out of her mind. Such a happening was by no means rare. People would be waiting for her and looking out for her in vain. Sometimes even a promise to lead a meeting would be forgotten. And not uncommonly business that had been entrusted to her would be completely overlooked. Sometimes she would buy tea at the tea market and then put it away out of sight where it would be left. When eventually she remembered it, it could no longer be used. It was not that she failed to appreciate the limitation of our resources but that other affairs would drive them from her mind. I too am apt to forget things but I have ways to repair this deficiency. When I agree to do anything for anybody I immediately record it on my engagement calendar. I also provided my wife with an engagement calendar but not only did she fail to write down her engagements, she might also fail to turn the pages for ten days or more. I regard punctuality as of extreme importance, but my wife is often late in attending meetings or keeping engagements. I felt that this was setting a bad example to others and it grieved me.

Another reason for the friction that sometimes arose between us was my hasty temperament. Sometimes I would pass on matters that I had only heard from others but not confirmed; sometimes I would exaggerate; sometimes I would show lack of sympathy and sensitiveness. Whenever my wife hears me speak in this way, no matter whether other people are present or not, she immediately corrects me. I was quite prepared for her to reprimand me in private but I did not accept that she should embarrass me in front of others. But she took the view that since it was in front of others that I had spoken unwisely it was right for her to correct me in front of others. I gradually came to realize that I truly needed someone to correct my faults in that way. And in order to avoid that kind of embarrassment I had to be more careful in what I said.

I must, however, warn those who read this that my wife should not necessarily be taken as a model in this respect. According to the Bible, when we see that a brother is at fault we should first of all exhort him alone (Matthew 18: 15-17). That is because we are all creatures of flesh and blood and there are times when we must allow for 'face'. To correct someone over-hastily can easily inflame his shame and vexation into anger, and when you do this you are no longer in a position to help him; on the contrary you may harm him. Where wives are concerned they should not necessarily follow the pattern of my wife. Her husband has accepted this kind of correction but not all husbands can do so. Because my wife knows that her husband will receive this kind of reprimand she knows that she can go ahead and act in this way. But this is not necessarily always the right course to follow. If you rashly imitate my wife you may be attempting more than you have the ability to achieve (you may attempt to make the picture of a tiger and only achieve the likeness of a dog) and give rise to other untoward incidents. When you imitate other people don't look only at the outward circumstances, give thought also to inner factors.

A positive attitude

I thank God that when I was fourteen he gave me a 'remonstrating friend' who helped me along the first stretch in the pathway of life. I thank God even more that when I was twenty-eight He gave me a 'remonstrating wife'. Throughout the years of my work for God she has given me immeasurable help and admonition. Whenever she saw my mistakes or my faults, whether in word or action, she would speak out. I know that there are wives who are blind to their husbands' faults and mistakes; and even when they do see them they are unwilling to point them out. If other people speak to the detriment of their husbands they become vexed and angry and fall out with them. My wife has never at any time covered my shortcomings and in this respect I have been tremendously helped by her.

I have a stormy disposition. I also have deep emotions. When I see a person with many good qualities I love him and am willing to do anything for him. And when I see a man with many shortcomings I dislike him and would like to banish him from my presence. But my wife often steps in and reminds me: 'When you see a man with good qualities you ought to remember that he also has shortcomings; and when you see a man with shortcomings you ought to remember that he also has good qualities. Everyone has both good qualities and shortcomings. We ourselves are no different.' When I am reprimanded like this my attitude towards other people is greatly changed.

My wife has yet another very special characteristic. Whenever she hears anyone being criticized she invariably constitutes herself the honorary advocate to act on his behalf and to defend him. Obviously defending people in this way can often be taken too far. But it remains true that very often it serves to reduce the bad feeling against the person in question and it de-pressurizes anger. It serves also to eliminate conflict. When a person speaks out angrily about others, if another person present speaks unhelpfully it is like pouring oil on a fire. But if someone counsels restraint, it is like pouring over the fire a pail of water. Far too many wives are well practised in throwing oil on the flames of their husband's anger, with the result that both get burnt. Take a person with a stormy disposition like me. If I had a wife accustomed to throwing oil on the flames of my anger I dare not imagine what calamities I should have provoked.

Before I was married I did not consider myself to be weak in the quality of love. But after I had lived with my wife for a number of years I came to realize that I was selfish and self-centred. I loved what was loveable but I did not love what was unloveable. My wife on the other hand is equally kind to all. I was always happy to help others provided it did not involve me in too much loss or inconvenience. But if it involved loss or inconvenience I could not act without a struggle. But my wife is ready at all times and in all places to sacrifice her own pleasure or advantage in order to help others. And this is done quite naturally without her having to force herself to do it. She once said to me, 'Although you do not harm others in order to benefit yourself, you are nevertheless selfish and self-seeking.' What she said was quite true.

But twenty years of instruction have enabled me to make a measure of progress.

My wife is always extremely considerate of others. If she gets up first in the morning she will move around very quietly and always speak in whispers so that she will not awaken others. I for my part have never had this habit but after years of training I am now making some progress. My wife is most unwilling to embarrass people. So only rarely does she address people with hasty words or with a stern countenance. Apart from the people whom she knows intimately, she is reluctant to reprove people. As for me I have only to see a believer do something wrong and I immediately reprove him without respect for his feelings. Because of this many people tend to stand in awe of me. But they have no such feeling towards my wife.

When my wife wants to do something for someone, she says nothing about it beforehand. When the time comes to do it she does it. When she wants to give things to people she tells no one about it beforehand and suddenly when least expected she makes her gifts. Sometimes she secretly puts things in people's houses and goes away. Or she puts things in people's handbags and only when they open their handbags do they find the gifts. They have no idea where they came from. I myself am quite different. If I want to do anything for anybody I promise beforehand that I will do it. Sometimes I cannot carry out my promise and people are disappointed. In this respect I have been greatly helped by my wife and I am gradually learning, even now, not to speak about such things beforehand. In this way, if I am able to do it, when the time comes I give people pleasure that they had not expected. If, on the other hand, I cannot do it, I do not cause people disappointment. Nor do I lose credibility with people.

I am a person given to anxiety and grief. Every day my heart is occupied by sadness and anxiety and trouble and fear. My wife on the other hand is able to leave things with the Lord no matter how serious they are. She does not need to kneel down and pray, but in her heart she quietly puts everything in the hands of God and she is no longer anxious about it. She commits her way to the Lord, and the Lord brings it to pass. So there is little heaviness in her heart and she faces every day with a smile. My wife's outlook has gradually influenced mine.

Complementing one another

I never mind using my strength or spending my money for other people. What I do not like, after using my strength and spending my money, is being misunderstood. But my wife is unconcerned about this. She says, 'People may misunderstand as they will, but so long as what I do does not offend God I am content.' It is strange when I stop to think about it. My wife certainly has some shortcomings. But the good qualities she has are mostly lacking in me. So God has used her to teach me many lessons.

When it comes to patience, I am left hopelessly behind my wife (lit. to see the dust raised by the person in front but to be unable to catch him up). Not infrequently we have callers who lack common-sense. They have no important business but they stay several hours. In spite of this my wife is never impatient. On one occasion a mentally unbalanced person came and talked with her and brought up a certain matter over and over again. On her first visit she stayed for several hours, and on the second visit she stayed for more than half a day. But my wife quietly and patiently listened to all she said. Hardly anyone, I fear, would be able to endure a prolonged conversation like this. But my wife said, 'This girl has experienced too much bitterness; she needs someone to give her a little sympathy and comfort.'

My wife never had the habit of reading. During the early years of our marriage I realized that because she lacked this habit there was a good deal of general knowledge she did not possess. Nor did she pay much attention to world events. Because of this I tended to look down on her. But I discovered later that she was far cleverer than I was. She quickly sums up a situation and is ready to meet any exigency. She is nimble-minded and can deal with situations that come upon you suddenly. In view of this, whenever I am faced with a situation which requires me to act, I first talk it over with her. She on her part makes many excellent suggestions. I often jokingly refer to her as my Chief of Staff. And when she went south to stay with her mother it was as if I had lost an arm.

At one time I gave little attention to the matter of eating and sleeping. From early morning until late afternoon I could carry on my work without stopping to eat. I was often absorbed in work at my desk, writing or attending to business until deep into the night. But my wife was different. If she passed much time without eating, her whole body would become weak and void of strength. If her sleep was inadequate she would suffer from headache. Because of this she gave particular attention to my own eating and sleeping habits. When she saw me neglecting meals and working late at night she often intervened. She said, 'To destroy your body is to destroy the temple of God.' At first I felt that she was intruding on my freedom and I got angry with her. Sometimes I would quarrel with her. But after I had twice been seriously ill I understood that a person who neglects eating and sleeping as I did needs a wife like this to intrude on his freedom. Otherwise by doing as he pleases he will destroy his own health and he will fail to complete the days that God has appointed for him. I have known quite a few people in this category.

Looking back over a few years we may say that friction between my wife and myself has at times been fairly fierce. There was one long period when we clashed almost daily. Whereas we were completely of one mind in important matters, we tended to quarrel about trivial matters. Each of us had a strong personality and when we were in conflict neither was willing to give way. Thank God He wanted to use this to rub off our corners so that we might both become 'smooth stones'.

Alas! In the case of many couples as soon as there is friction they begin to talk of divorce. They feel that by separating they will reduce their suffering, whereas in actual fact they are forfeiting much happiness. In addition to that they fall into many sins and many sorrows. God does not allow those who belong to Him to divorce each other in this way. Yet this restriction is not to take away their freedom. It is in order that they might be happy. Suppose it was not against God's law for a couple to divorce each other as they wish, and suppose we two had divorced each other when the friction between us was fiercest, where would we be today?

If there are couples at odds with each other amongst those who are reading this I urge you to look away to God, to be patient and to obey Him. Sooner or later you will experience God's wonderful grace. When the small (rough) stones have become smooth stones you will understand what a blessed thing it is to obey God.

It is nearly 22 years since my wife and I were married. Although we once passed through a long period of friction we still maintained our trust in each other. We did not tell each other lies, nor did we harbour suspicions about each other. We did not deceive each other. We were loyal in our friendship and sincere in our relationship.

My original ideal for a wife was of a woman excelling in literary matters. In that way she could be my secretary. However, my wife is not that kind of person. Even when she writes a letter of sufficient importance to have to use literary language she needs my help to make a rough draft. Nevertheless whenever necessary she can correct my manuscripts. She is not able to preach but after I have preached she can tell me where my phraseology or my arrangement has been faulty. She is not a competent housewife but she is an excellent fellow-worker. She is not an experienced secretary, skilled in managing affairs in the office. But she is a fine proof-reader both in my work and in my life. She is not what I originally conceived of as the ideal wife but she is the perfect partner. I now understand that my original ideal was imperfect and that my original understanding was faulty. Now more than ever I believe in what God

Himself has stated.

'For my thoughts are not your thoughts, neither are your ways my ways,' saith the Lord. For as the heavens are higher than the earth, so are my ways higher than your ways, and my thoughts than your thoughts.' (Isaiah 55:8,9)

9.
Memories of my Mother...

On October 18th, 1947, my mother passed away peacefully at No. 29 Gan-yu Lane, Peking.

My mother was not highly intelligent, but her memory was fairly strong. Even when she was over 80 she could still recite from the classics the passages she had learnt in childhood. Her temperament was stormy. Once she decided in her mind that a particular circumstance was to be viewed in a certain way, no one could change it. As a child I frequently contradicted her. She did not wish to reprove me but she would lose her temper and break things. When she had to discuss matters with neighbours in our courtyard, on eight or nine occasions out of ten she would lose her temper. In this respect my sister and I

203

took very much after mother. If God had not changed me I truly do not know what I should be like today.

My mother's lot during my childhood was a very bitter one. Our food was always coarse. In winter-time our home was never warm enough. The clothes we wore were too thin; my mother's hands and mine were invariably cracked with cold and very painful.

During my school days I was often ill. Then my mother cared for me night and day. I always loved my mother but my mother's love for me was far greater. Even to think of her moves me to tears. When I was small my mother always took me to school because she feared that I would be exposed to danger on the way. I did not like my school-mates to see this lest they should think me weak and powerless. So I objected to mother escorting me. She solved the problem by compromising — she followed me at a distance.

When I was small the three of us in the family had only one small room. Having been at school I knew that fresh air had a considerable bearing on health, so I suggested that while we were sleeping we should leave the window open. But my mother believed in the old method of keeping the windows closed lest we get cold at night and thus become seriously ill. I clashed with my mother many times over this. In order not to make me unhappy, and still protect her children from the cold, my mother adopted the practice of waiting until we were asleep before she closed the windows and of opening them before we woke up. But I woke up early and saw what my mother was doing so I clashed with her again.

Personal attachment

After I became a Christian, when I was fourteen, I became more sensitive and began to sympathize more with my mother. When I was 17 the school moved to another part of the city which was farther from home. I was always concerned about my mother's health but I now began to fear that she would die. The new school building had four storeys and from the windows higher up you could see many houses all round and you could also hear many of the sounds of the neighbourhood. The people were mostly poor people. Every time anyone died the people would hang white paper outside the house and they would engage musicians to play small trumpets. Every time I heard the sound of these trumpets I had a fear in my heart that my mother had died. My anxiety lasted until the following Saturday when I hurried home to find my mother still alive and well. Only then did I relax. Even so I would post a letter home on Tuesday or Wednesday to enquire whether my mother was well or not.

In the spring of 1921 when I had to return to my home after being forced to leave Baoding it was a great disappointment and a heavy blow to my mother. One evening from my own room I heard my mother crying in the room opposite, 'I'll go mad! I'll go mad! I can't bear it!' When I heard this my heart was pierced as by a sword. I feared then that my mother would become mentally ill. For on one occasion, after a brawl with the neighbours, her nerves became disordered and she went out on the street without knowing where she was. I loved my mother so much, I was so concerned about her health, and I was so unwilling to see her suffer that I decided to put on one side the commission that God had given me and to follow the path pleasing to my mother. But the Lord then spoke to me through a passage of Scripture: 'He who loves his father or mother more than me is nor worthy of me.' How could I therefore abandon God's commission out of sympathy for my mother? That was utterly impossible! Even if through this she became mentally ill I could never turn my back on the Lord. Thank God! He is truly faithful. He tested me at that time in the same way He had tested Abraham of old. Abraham, in order to obey God, gave up his only son Isaac. But God preserved Isaac so that he received no harm whatever. So with me. I gave up the mother I loved but God preserved her. She had a spell of weeping, but all passed by peacefully and without incident. Nor did she, because of my actions, become mentally ill.

When God increased the scope of my ministry in 1925 He met all my needs, according to His promise, through those who belonged to Him. This enabled me to support my mother. I was also able to hire a servant-girl to do the chores in the home which I had been doing when I was without employment. Conditions for my mother improved greatly.

In the winter of 1925 I spent a considerable period working in the province of Jejiang (south of the River Yangtze). Because of fighting at that time the railway communications were cut both north and south of the river. Letters between Shanghai and Peking took five or six days. Every few days I sent a letter home, but rarely did I receive a letter from home. For my mother to write was extremely difficult. And my sister did not like writing letters. I did not hear for many days and I was concerned about my mother's health. Once in a dream I returned home and saw a coffin there and I was told that my mother had died. It brought me great sorrow. Only when I awoke did I realize that it was just a dream. Night after night my dreams were filled with unpropitious happenings and throughout the same period I received no news from home. I sent a telegram but I received no reply. I decided that my mother must have died and that my sister was afraid to tell me. I almost had a mental breakdown. I couldn't eat and I couldn't sleep. I then sent a telegram to Mrs Pan. A few days later I had a telegram from my sister who told me that my mother was well and that all at home was peaceful. I finally relaxed.

Even when I was over forty my mother continued to admonish me in the same way that she had admonished me when I was a child. When I had to travel anywhere she would urge me not to go near mountain peaks and other places of danger and to be careful when boarding or alighting from trains. In order to allay my mother's fears I would always send letters or postcards frequently and sometimes, after a long journey, would send a telegram on reaching my destination.

A new home

After the completion of the Tabernacle in 1937 and the adding of accommodation in the courtyard there, my wife and I moved across and made our home there. The old home, where my mother and sister lived, became more peaceful, and I was much better placed to carry out my responsibilities at the church. So long as I was in Peking I went to the old home every day. My wife also paid frequent visits to my mother and sister. The misunderstanding, however, was not removed.

Sister's death

In March, 1946, I made the long trip to the south-west, expecting to stay for two months. For several reasons my stay was extended to five months. I finally returned to Peking, via Shanghai, in August. Shortly before my arrival, on the evening of the 17th, my sister was taken ill. I had been away for a long time and a great deal of business had accumulated. Also we were about to begin evangelistic meetings for university students. So I could not serve my sister properly for some days. My mother also became ill, and because of her age I feared that she would not easily recover. Before my sister died she had already changed her attitude to my wife. On the afternoon before she died she said, 'I am holding God's hand.'

After the death of my sister I thought that my mother would perhaps change her attitude to my wife. On the contrary it became worse. Eventually we thought it wise for my wife to visit her less frequently. I would go along daily taking my son when I could. When my mother became ill I would stay there at night. She still lamented the loss of my sister. Sometimes believers would visit her but she never lost her suspicion of them. Because of my work at the church, and my work in connection with The Spiritual Food Quarterly, and other responsibilities, I could not always be at my mother's side. For more than a year after the death of my sister, however, I made no trips outside Peking apart from two short trips to Tienjin and two to the Province of Shansi.

My mother was really very blessed in that her son had been chosen by God to do His work. But she did not appreciate this. She lamented that I had not become a successful business man and become wealthy. Believers would sometimes tell her that her son's work was more important than that of the president of a country. But she would reply, 'Too laborious! Too wearisome!"

If only she could have appreciated the importance of the work in which her son was engaged. How happy she could have been. But she didn't. And this was her loss. It was also her sorrow.

10.
We must obey God rather than men...

(This final chapter does not come at the end chronologically, but it is a fitting conclusion. It throws considerable light on our brother's character).

At the beginning of August in 1939 (which was the third year of the Japanese occupation of North China) I returned to my home in Peking after ministry in Hongkong. I was shown, on arrival, a document sent out by the Japanese Ministry of Information. It was a directive requiring all newspapers and periodicals published in the city to insert, in their next issue, four slogans drawn up by the Japanese Army Bureau. Anyone daring to disobey this directive would be severely punished. The brother who handed it to me also voiced his opinion. Obviously, he said, we cannot publish slogans like this; but not to publish them is certainly dangerous. Who would dare to disregard a direction from the Japanese military? At the time I weakened. While I was determined not to compromise truth by publishing God-dishonouring slogans I did not possess the courage to publish our periodical (The Spiritual Food Quarterly) in the usual way without including the slogans. I discussed the matter with several believers and with one voice they recommended that we let the Spiritual Food Quarterly cease publication voluntarily. In this way we would avoid compromising truth and yet at the same time avoid incurring danger. In view of my having weakened I naturally welcomed advice like this and accordingly began my preparations to halt publication.

That year we had published a combined issue for Spring and Summer, but the Autumn issue had not yet been published. Subscriptions covered the whole year, so if publication ceased half-way through the year I would have to return subscriptions for the second half of the year. So I prepared to print and distribute an announcement informing subscribers that we would either refund the half-year subscription or send books to that value. While I was making these preparations my heart was full of anguish, because up to that time the Spiritual Food Quarterly had been published for twelve and a half years. In fact I regarded this publication as my child. Every quarter I myself wrote the manuscript; I corrected it; and sometimes I even sent it out. Many readers had told me of help that they had received through reading this periodical. But publication was now to be halted. The child was dying an early death. My heart was filled with great sorrow.

On August 14th, in the evening, I was praying in my room when suddenly my heart was rebuked by the Holy Spirit. I asked myself some questions. 'When you began publishing the Spiritual Food Quarterly did you not do so because you were unmistakably guided by God? And during the twelve and a half years of its publication is it not true that many have been helped by it? Who is it that today is causing you to stop publication? It is not that God is causing you to stop publication, but that you yourself are voluntarily ceasing publication because of an order issued by the Information Ministry of the Japanese Army. Is not this a case of fleeing as you approach the scene of battle? If we publish those slogans we shall be raising the white flag of surrender to Satan; but if we decide voluntarily to cease publication would it not be a far bigger surrender than publishing the slogans?' Come what may, we cannot halt publication. We need not enquire as to hypothetical dangers in the future, we will go ahead and publish the periodical as usual but we will not insert the slogans.

After prayer I felt strengthened and prepared to act. I pondered the fact that to publish the magazine without the slogans would almost inevitably bring trouble, for at that time we were required to hand over several copies of every issue to government officials. If the Ministry of Information of the Japanese Army discovered this omission it was absolutely certain that they would be extremely angry. For in their eyes this would amount to disobeying their orders. The outlook was distinctly sombre. If they reacted leniently we would at least expect instructions to cease publication; but if they reacted harshly they would probably arrest me and charge me with various crimes. But I determined not to be swayed by these considerations and resolved to stand firm to see the matter through. They might compel us to cease publication but we would not cease publication voluntarily. Whatever dangers might arise and whatever we might be called upon to suffer I would not abandon the task that God had committed to me.

I knew that God had chosen me to use me and that in the grave situation in which we were placed He relied on me to be loyal. As the saying is, 'A soldier is trained for a thousand days; he is used only briefly.' This was the time that God wanted to use me and on no account must I flee as we approached the battle.

The next day I discussed my decisions with several fellow-believers. No one was willing to utter an opinion. On the one hand they did not wish to hinder me yet on the other hand they hesitated to express approval. Afterwards I shared my thinking with my wife. She asked me, 'Are you prepared to be arrested, to be examined, and to be jailed by them? If you are not fully prepared for these things I fear that when the time comes you won't be able to endure it. But if you are prepared for these things you may screw up your courage and go.' I replied right away, 'I am prepared.' She said, 'Then you may go and act according to what God has shown you.' Thank God, this is just what I did. The Spiritual Food Quarterly was published as usual. Not one word did we publish of the slogans that the Japanese military had ordered us to insert in this issue. After publication we sent a copy for them to scrutinize as usual. What happened? They did not arrest me. They did not instruct me to cease publication. They did not even communicate with me. The Japanese Army occupied North China for eight years yet at no time was the Spiritual Food Quarterly adulterated (that is, with political matter). Like Daniel I can say, 'My God sent his angel, and he shut the mouths of the lions. They have not hurt me . . .'

Churches closing

The fiercest fighting took place in the spring of 1942. In December 1941 Japan had declared war on Britain and America. On that morning all the places of worship established by British and American missionary societies were closed and sealed. On Sunday, December 14th, very few chapels in the city were open for normal worship. This was the first time since the Boxer Rising of 1900 that the large chapels had halted worship services. The leaders of all the churches were extremely anxious. They discussed ways of continuing the work and for this purpose they set up a 'Peking Church Committee' informing every church by circular letter. On December 17th the Christians' Tablernacle situated at 42 Shih-chia Hutung, which is the meeting place of the church that I took care of, duly received a letter which read as follows:

It was decided today that on the 18th of this month (Thursday) at 3 o'clock in the afternoon in the large ceremonial hall of the head office of the Ministry of Home Affairs a meeting will be convened to discuss necessary arrangements to operate a "Christian Church Preservation Committee". It is hoped that you will be present at the appointed time.

— The Peking Christian Preservation Committee
December 15.

It occurred to me when I received this letter that the procedure adopted by the churches was exactly like the Israelites' call for help as they went down to Egypt. By seeking help from the Japanese the churches gave the Japanese an opportunity to use them. They (the leaders of the churches) should have looked only to God and not to seek help from the Japanese. For no matter what the nature of the business, as soon as you seek help from men you cannot avoid accepting the conditions they impose. The path that these churches were treading was basically so different from the path that I was treading that there was in fact no way for me to help them. Our church had had no connection with any missionary society and thus far our buildings had not been closed and sealed; so there was really no need for us to be involved with the 'Preservation Committee'. There was no point in our attending the meeting.

From that time on although I heard here and there a little news of the Christian Preservation Committee I did not pay much attention to it. This situation continued until January 16th in the following year (1942). A believer then paid me a visit out of the blue informing me that the churches had already set up a 'North China Christian Federation Promotion Committee', and he had been deputed by the chairman to urge us to participate. He pointed out that if we failed to participate then in all probability the church would subsequently encounter difficulties. Truly I did not know, on the spur of the moment, how to reply. I simply told him that I would let him have a reply in the evening. That evening I discussed the matter with my wife and two church colleagues, and with another brother. We all knelt to pray. Within a few minutes a passage in the Bible came to my mind: 'What part hath he that believeth with an infidel?' (2 Corinthians 6:15). I ceased my supplications; I could only give thanks and praise because it was already clear to me how I should handle the situation. God had forbidden me to be yoked together with unbelievers. Many of the members of those churches had not yet truly repented and believed; moreover there were even pastors who had never repented and believed. God would not allow me to be yoked together with them. What the leaders in many of these churches were preaching not only failed to edify people it was actually destroying people's faith. Many churches abounded in features opposed to the truth; they had merged with the world. God would now allow me to be yoked together with them.

We also perceived that the 'North China Christian Federation Promotion Committee' now had a political background, being used by the Japanese. God would not allow me to be yoked together with those taking part.

At the end of our prayer time I asked what conclusions the others had come to. All five of us 'with different mouths but with one voice' had come to the conclusion that we should not take part. So that evening we sent a reply to the one who had contacted us informing him what we had decided.

The next day one of my colleagues (the one who had conveyed our decision the night before) pointed out that, based on the reaction when he conveyed our reply, the Committee regarded participation as compulsory. Irrespective of whether one wanted to join or not, joining was essential. It was not a matter of choice. Further, our continued existence as a church depended on our joining. I had the feeling that I and my colleagues were like the captain and first and second officers of a steamer, that the vessel was whipped by violent gales and buffeted by heavy seas, and that the safety or otherwise of the whole ship (the whole church) depended entirely on us few officers. Our responsibility was heavy in the extreme; we only needed to make one mistake and the whole ship would be plunged to the bottom of the sea. On the 18th I spoke myself to the man who had originally been in contact with us and told him that since our church had decided not to join the Federation Promotion Committee we would advise the chairman of the Committee that he need not further enquire into our affairs.

At the beginning of March when I was engaged in ministry in Tientsin I received a letter from a fellow-worker who informed me that the Committee representative who had contacted us earlier had come again to talk with him, again urging us to join the Federation. He had replied: 'Mr Wong is not in Peking; I cannot take responsibility in his absence.'

An example to follow . . . . .

On July 7th I returned from Tientsin to Peking just in time to meet a sister who had come from the Province of Anhwei in order to see me. I learned from her that the Girls' School of which she was Principal had been taken over by the Japanese, and that the Japanese authorities had put pressure on her to continue as Principal and to help them run the school. She had replied saying that she could not co-operate with unbelievers. And although the Japanese both enticed her and threatened her, from beginning to end she had refused to co-operate. Finally they took her to the Military Police, but she would not budge in the slightest. And there was nothing they could do about it. After I had listened to her testimony my faith was quickened and my resolve was strengthened. I pondered the implications. Here was a woman who courageously refused to yield and who remained faithful to God. And here was I, a man, who was the leader of a church — a man, moreover, who had received a solemn commission from God — how could I of all people submit to the pressure of evil forces? As a result of the conversation with that sister I was considerably strengthened, and my resolve not to join the Federation, no matter what the outcome, was strongly reinforced.

. . . . . and to avoid

On April 18th I attended a funeral service and I there met a Japanese pastor. After the funeral service he made every effort to persuade me to join the Federation mentioning that Mr Takeda of the Asian Prosperity Bureau was anxious to talk to me. He also added: 'The Federation Promotion Committee needs men of strong will like you to take part in it.' I replied, 'It's just because I am strong minded that I have decided not to participate.' The two of us stood talking in the street for an hour.

On April 19th I preached in our church on the theme of the saints who had experienced in some cases the fiery furnace and in one case the lion's den. At that time I greatly feared the threatened danger and I preached on that subject partly to encourage others and partly to encourage myself.

The pressure increases

In the evening of April 30th, when I returned from outside and came in for the evening meal, my wife gave me a letter. It was from the Federation Promotion Committee and this is what it said:

In view of recent developments and in order to advance the true spirit of self-support, self-control and self-propagation in the churches, we who represent various denominations and groups of the Christian Church are in process of setting up the North China Christian Federation Promotion Committee. A central office was formally established on April 18th and according to regulations we ought to set up a branch office in this city. Since your esteemed meeting hall is located within the boundary of this branch it becomes necessary for you to join the Committee. We particularly request you to send a representative to be present on May 1st at 10 o'clock in the morning to discuss plans for progress. The meeting place is the Christian Church at x.

Peking Branch Office,
The North China Christian Federation
Promotion Committee.

During the previous three or four months, although the Federation Promotion Committee had repeatedly exhorted me, they had always commissioned someone to come and talk to me. But this time it was a written communication that was delivered and this stated clearly 'Participation is essential'. Further, we had to give them a formal written reply. So this time we could not avoid crossing swords. That evening, at half past nine, after everyone else had gone to bed, I sat alone on the platform on the south side of the chapel thinking the matter over. By the old calendar it was the 16th day of the 3rd month, and the moon shone very brightly over the whole courtyard. I called to mind the period of ten years or so that had passed, and the way in which God had led me; how we began with a small gathering of two or three people in my house and how we had gradually grown, first to several tens, and then to one or two hundred. I recalled how we had rented accommodation for meetings and how later, on the present site, we had bought land and erected a building; how numbers increased to four or five hundred. With this present convenient chapel we need no longer be anxious about the accommodation being too small or the people too many. I also pondered how during the past years God had taken care of the church, and how in every department there had been considerable progress. All the belivers in the church and my several co-workers were of one heart and mind working together for the advance of the gospel. Yet we were now facing a time of crisis.

To join this Babylon-like North China Christian Federation Promotion Committee would for me be disobeying the will of God. Yet not to join would inevitably bring Japanese intervention. The church would probably be closed and I personally would find it difficult to escape danger. I also thought of my aging mother. If she were to hear that I had been arrested she would certainly be anxious and fearful, wondering what calamity might arise. I was clearly aware that for anyone to show unwillingness to obey the Japanese military would bring unwelcome results.

Further, they would probably occupy our chapel and

use it for some other purpose. No longer would it be possible for several hundred believers to meet each week and joyfully worship God together. With the pastor in confinement the flock would be scattered. As I turned these things over in my mind a great conflict arose; I could not think any more, nor could I bring my thinking to a conclusion. I realised that if I wanted to avoid these tragic consequences I would have to submit and join the Federation. But if I did that I would have to make common cause with those whom I had previously rebuked; the friction would drag on interminably; while superficially one we would differ widely in outlook (sleeping in one bed, but each having his own dreams); while divided in heart we would have discussions as if we were one. I would have to co-operate with some who 'looked upon piety as a means to profit'. In my heart I would see things that were wrong but with my mouth I would have to say they were all right. I would have to acknowledge black as white; to point at a deer and call it a horse; I would have to pack away my faith and my principles in a cupboard.

If I joined the Federation I would have to consign many of the letters and articles I had written to the flames. I have strongly maintained that the church could not allow its activities to merge with worldly customs and that God's workers cannot co-operate with false prophets and false teachers. I have always maintained that churches which stand for the truth of 'salvation through faith (and by grace)' cannot be affiliated with associations or groups that do not believe these truths. It also became clear to me that if I joined this Federation I would inevitably overthrow the testimony which I had borne all over China throughout the past twenty years. God's name would

be greatly dishonoured by my action and countless believers would be stumbled. How could I allow myself to do this? How could I be a traitor to the Lord whom I had served for over twenty years? I could never be happy to be a disciple of Judas. These are the things that I pondered that night in the moonlight; — I then went into the small meeting room and knelt down to pray. After praying I went back into the moonlight and pondered the situation again and then once again to pray in the small meeting room. I moved backwards and forwards in this way many times. Normally when I am praying by myself I hardly ever open my mouth, but that night I prayed in a loud voice, so much so that all my fellow-workers sleeping upstairs heard me clearly. I had a taste that night of the Lord's experience in Gethsemane. Not until 2 o'clock in the morning did I lie down on my bed. Thank God, He came to my aid; that night, He gave me strength, He gave me faith and courage, so that I was able to make a resolution on no account to join the 'Federation Promotion Committee'. That night I slept only four hours and even in my sleep I continued without intermission to dream about the things on my mind. In the early morning I wrote a letter and handed it over to the church messenger to take to the Promotion Committee of the Federation. This is what I wrote:

I acknowledge the receipt of your letter directing me to join the North China Christian Federation Promotion Committee. On examining your statement with its references to Western Missions and to the objective of becoming self-supporting, self-governing and self-propagating, I conclude that it is not necessary for us to join your group. In addition to that your Federation is made up of churches of different faith from ours, and in order to preserve an unadulterated faith it would be difficult for us to affiliate with churches of different faith. Consequently we are unable to follow your directions and to send a representative to your meeting. I hope that you will understand our position.

That morning a Christian came to see me who was the delegate of a church which had joined the Federation. He told me that the gatekeeper had brought in my letter just as they were meeting. After they had read it they acknowledged that no one could hope to influence a man so stubborn as myself. All that they could do was to hand the letter over to the Japanese and let them handle the matter. Later in their meeting a Japanese came in and the letter was handed over to him. After reading it he put it in his pocket. At the close of the meeting he went out and took a northerly direction. In all probability, thought my informant, he had gone to the headquarters of the Japanese Army. My caller then urged me to take immediate steps to restore the situation which was now very grave. He urged me on no account to upset the Japanese Army authorities because that would be extremely dangerous. He pressed me to join the Federation without delay while there was still time. I answered that my mind was already made up and that I had resolved not to join. I thanked him for his kind consideration but explained that I was unable to accept his advice. Seeing that my mind was made up he made the comment: 'Each one has his own gift and each one has his own interpretation. Since your mind is made up I will not persist in urging you to join. However, nothing need hinder you from talking to Mr Kawano (a Japanese) to avoid unnecessary misunderstandings.' He then gave me Mr Kawano's address and telephone number.

A moment of weakness

After he had gone I reflected on his suggestion and agreed that such a course would not be amiss. So I decided to seek out a believer who could speak Japanese to come with me as interpreter. But when I discussed the proposition with my wife she disagreed with me: 'Why do you want to go and see Mr Kawano? He is not looking for you, and if you first go looking for him it will indicate that you are afraid of his misunderstanding you. We have decided not to affiliate and we have legitimate reasons for our attitude. You have no reason whatever to go and call on him.' Since my wife opposed my going I modified my attitude somewhat. It was Friday, and every Friday evening we met together for Bible study. A believer who could speak Japanese almost invariably attended that meeting, so I decided that if she came that evening I would go ahead with the suggested visit to Mr Kawano; but if she failed to turn up I would take that as guidance that God was stopping us. In the event she did not attend that evening, so the idea of visiting Mr Kawano was dropped.

More pressure

On June 24th in the evening a brother who regularly attended our meetings came and talked to me. News had reached him, he said, that in accordance with Japanese instructions the local government authorities had decided to close all churches not affiliated with the Federation. He continued: 'Almost all the churches in the city have joined the Federation; why are you so determined not to join?' He felt that I was obstinately holding to personal opinion. And the closing of the church would be extremely regrettable.

He testified that when he first came to Peking he had visited many places of worship in his search for a spiritual home, and that finally he had settled on us. If our church was now closed he would have nowhere to go. He urged me to join quickly and thus avoid the threatened danger. We then held a long conversation and I explained to him in detail the reasons for not joining. When he understood the reasons he added the comment: 'Since you have adequate reasons like this I can only counsel you to hold on firmly to the end.'

During the weeks following all kinds of unpleasant rumours came to my ears. It seemed that sooner or later our meeting place would be closed; also there was a group within the church itself who did not agree with what I was doing. They were taken up with the realisation that the closing of the church would be a most unwelcome development and did not appreciate that joining the Federation involved disobeying God. At a meeting of believers on June 28th I explained how joining the Federation could not be harmonised with maintaining the truth; it was therefore better to close than to join the Federation. Throughout that whole period I never lost the feeling that every meeting might be our last one.

We were once informed of a statement made by a Japanese pastor to the effect that any church refusing to join the Federation was guilty of a 'Chungking Connection'. I imagined that this indicated a crime which could not be expurgated. In the war between Japan on the one hand and Britain and America on the other all churches related to Britain or America were designated 'Enemy Connection Churches'. Since our church had not originated from Britain or America and since we received no support from British or

American missionary societies they could not accuse us of being a 'British Connection' or an 'American Connection' church. But I was a Chinese, so they charged us with being 'Chungking Connection' (Chunking being the war-time capital of China). How could a crime like this be expurgated? The feeling persisted that danger lay immediately ahead of us and not unnaturally we could not avoid a measure of anxiety. But in spite of apprehension we had already made up our mind, and this meant that our hearts were free from conflict.

As the days went by, rumours became more numerous and the situation more tense. So much so that some of those who had attended church regularly now began to drop off. Among them was one man who stated openly that he had ceased to attend through fear of being arrested. But what would the Japanese arrest him for? It could truly be said in those days that 'Rumours were the songs of cranes; wood and grass were soldiers.' Many people were anxious on my behalf. Moreover several believers in distant places who heard of the situation sent me letters urging me to join the Federation and avoid danger. Every time I received a letter of this nature I regarded it as an exhortation of the kind that Peter once used when the Lord answered him: 'Thou savourest not the things that be of God, but those that be of men.'

Thank God He protected me and prevented me from doubting His guidance and from being shaken in my original resolve. I thank Him specially that He opened my eyes to see that many saints are caused to stumble and to sin through fear. I perceived that King Saul fell from his high position to a state of misery because at the outset he saw that the Philistines were great in number and his heart was gripped by fear. He also rebelled against God (1 Samuel 13:1-15). It was plain that various churches had joined the Federation through fear of the Japanese. I also reflected that Saul was rejected by God and that he was not again worthy to be a servant of God. I realised that I was then in danger of falling into a state of misery like Saul. Having derived help from the history of Saul I chose this subject to preach on during the summer convention held that year during the period August 3-16.

During August and September the North China Christian Federation Promotion Committee title changed again. In Japan itself the title of the organization unifying the churches had already been changed to 'Japan Christian Association'. The Japanese now initiated a change of the title in China from 'North China Christian Federation' to 'North China Christian Association'.* The officers of the organization did not at first approve of it, for it was not a Bible expression and it was obviously being manipulated by the Japanese, but since the Japanese insisted on their putting into practice the policies they had drawn up, and there was no one in the Federation Promotion Committee strong enough to oppose it, they finally accepted it. Following this on August 8th the Ministry of Home Affairs called together the leaders of all the churches and of a Women's Bible School to attend a conference to establish the Association. The conference was to last three days. When I heard of this I felt that the day for our church to be closed was relentlessly approaching, and I took special pains to urge the believers to be strong and courageous, to act as soldiers of Christ, and on no account to yield to the forces of evil.

The climax of the conflict

The crucial battle was indeed about to take place. At 6 o'clock on October 9th the Japanese Mr Kawano and a Chinese interpreter came to see me at our place of meeting (which we called the Christians' Tabernacle) and informed me that the Investigating Officer of the North China Cultural Bureau (which was part of the Asian Prosperity Department) wanted to talk to me. He asked me if I could go to their office the next morning at 9 o'clock. I knew then that the final battle was immediately ahead. Both my own future work and the whole future of the Christians' Tabernacle were hanging on this impending conversation. I could not draw back; nor did I want to draw back. I therefore agreed to go. I recalled that earlier, on May 1st, I had refrained from seeking out Mr Kawano, but now, after the lapse of 5 months, here was Mr Kawano looking for me. The next morning (October 10th, 1942) several believers came to the Tabernacle specially to pray for me. Before 9 o'clock I set out on my bicycle. As I cycled along the road I opened my

* The expression which I have translated 'Association' uses the same two ideographs in both Japanese and Chinese, being pronounced kyōdan and 'jiao-twan' respectively. In Japanese it means in general 'a religious body' and specifically 'The United Church of Christ in Japan'. The combination of the two ideographs does not appear in my Chinese dictionary and was probably a novel expression to the Chinese church leaders when introduced by the Japanese. The general meaning would be recognized as 'a teaching group' or 'a religious group' but specialized meaning would still be taken from the context.

mouth and sang the hymn 'Stand up, stand up for Jesus.'

From victory unto victory   Put on the Gospel armour
His army shall He lead   And watching unto prayer
Till every foe is conquered   Where duty calls or danger
And Christ is Lord indeed   Be never wanting there

I could not restrain my exuberance. It was as if I was leading thousands of warriors into battle. I duly reached the office and met Mr Takeda. He first chatted about affairs in general and then he said: 'On the 15th of this month the North China Christian Association will be formally established; the Japanese and Chinese alike hope that you can exercise some leadership.' I said to him, 'Mr Takeda there are two things I would like you to know. The first is that I personally will on no account join any group or organization. The second is that the church for which I am responsible will on no account join any group or organization.' I then explained to him something of my beliefs, my principles, and my commission; and I gave my reasons for not joining any group or organization. He commented that I had very strong views. But he continued, 'The government has decided that all the churches will unite and it is essential that this policy be carried out.' I replied: 'In order that I may obey God whom I serve, in order that I may hold firmly the truth that I believe, I will on no account obey any instruction that cuts across Gods's will. I have prepared myself to pay any price, to make any sacrifice, and nothing will make me change these principles. It is out of the question for me or for my church to join the Association.' He then said, 'I beg you to think the matter over.' I replied, 'I have already thought the matter over for several months; it is unnecessary to think the matter over any more. He repeated his request many times and I insisted as many times that there was no further need to think it over. I realized that for me to answer in this way may have seemed hard and inflexible and left no room for saving face, but I could not tell lies. Having made up my mind not to think it over any longer I could not say that I would. Nor was I prepared to give him room to put further pressure on me. I had to take advantage of a time when I was feeling strong to cut off my line of retreat. If the church had to be closed, then so it had to be. If I had to be arrested, then so it had to be. By this time we had been talking for about an hour. 'Mr Takeda,' I said, 'If there is no other matter of importance, I will take my leave.' I stood up; he also stood up. He then took my hand very warmly. I did not, at the time, understand the significance of this friendly gesture. Was it because he had been moved by our conversation? Or was he expressing a good feeling before advising the military police to arrest me and punish me? I did not know. Whatever it was, God had certainly protected me throughout.

The next day was Sunday and we had meetings both in the morning and in the afternoon. It really seemed to me now that these would be the last meetings to be held on our premises. I had spoken with such forthrightness that no retreat was possible. We had refused to join the Association and how could we now avoid the closure of the church?

Four more days passed. Then the 'North China Chinese Christian Association' convened a large inaugural meeting. Four features of that meeting attracted our attention: (1) The inaugural meeting was not held in any church building, but in a Government building. (2) Japanese military and political chiefs in North China together with other important people from political councils were present on the platform and gave speeches of felicitation. (3) The 5th item on the programme read as follows: For the purpose of quiet meditation on the war dead among the officers and men from friendly States in great East Asia (though later, on the anniversary of that meeting, only the words 'quiet meditation' were printed). (4) On that day posters were put up all over the city with the words, 'New citizens' meeting. Congratulations on the inauguration of the 'North China Christian Association!'

We need not enquire into all that went on behind the scenes. Provided a man is not a simpleton he only needs to look at these four features and he will readily understand the background of the North China Christian Association. Quite a few in our own church who had not understood previously why I refused to join the Association have now come gradually to understand it.

The final test

At that time I had no means of visualizing changes that the future might bring, only that we were daily prepared to encounter untoward circumstances. On November 18th the local police brought a letter instructing me to go immediately to the office of the Japanese Military Police. From the time that the Japanese army had occupied Peking I had at no time received any communication from the Japanese Military Police. Now without warning I was summoned to their headquarters. I presumed that it had to do with the Church Association. I supposed that the Japanese would use the power of the Military Police to press me and threaten me; thus if I still did not submit they would first confine me and then deal with me. Not for a moment did I entertain the thought that the visit could be for any other reason. Consequently I quickly got my overcoat, packed my Bible, spectacle case, handkerchief, tooth brush and a pair of woollen socks. I put on two other garments and prepared myself for imprisonment. Whatever happened I was still determined not to join the Association. Not only did I promise before God that I would follow Him to the end, I also addressed my flock like this: 'If I one day yield and lead our church to affiliate with the North China Chinese Christian Association, then you must all immediately throw me over. Do not again listen to my preaching. You will call me Judas Iscariot.' These words were spoken at a meeting of believers on October 25th. I had already sunk the boats (burnt the boats); I had already cut off the escape route. As I was about to leave that day I said to my wife: 'If I have not returned home by sunset it means that I have been detained in custody by the Military Police. No matter what happens I shall not give in.'

I had long expected that the Military Police would one day arrest me, and I had said to my fellow-workers, 'If I am arrested by the Military Police, none of you must take steps for the church to join the Association in order to effect my release. If you act in this way, then when I come out I not only will refrain from thanking you, I shall blame you. And since we shall have incurred disgrace we had better voluntarily close our doors and cease to operate.'

On that particular day I said very little to my wife. When she escorted me to the door I set off without even turning my head. When I arrived at the Military Police headquarters I found that pastors from other churches were also there. When I enquired why they had come I learned that they had been summoned by the Military Police in regard to the handing over of property belonging to the Missionary Societies. Addressing my enquiry directly to the Military Police I elicited the information that the business had nothing to do with me; I had been summoned in error. So I returned home. Although it was a false alarm I realize on looking back that it was nevertheless very significant. The Lord had given strength according to need and had not allowed His name to be dishonoured.

From the time that Mr Kawano came to see me on October 10th no one had come to visit me from either the Japanese or the Church Association. For several months I was prepared at any time for possible danger and not until 1942 had passed did I reckon that the likelihood of further interrogation was fading.

In November 1943 I had occasion to go to Tsingtao to lead special meetings and one of the brothers there told me of remarks made by Mr Takeda when invited there by churches of the Association. One of those attending Association meetings asked a question: 'Mr Takeda, is it not required of the churches in North China that they join the Association? How is it then that the church pastored by Mr Wong Ming-dao does not join?' Mr Takeda replied: 'I once had a conversation with Mr Wong. He has ample reasons for not joining. His attitude moreover is very determined. We have no means of compelling him to join.' The questioner continued: 'If other churches took the same attitude and refused to join would not the Association be in fragments?' Mr Takeda replied: 'Other churches cannot act in this way.'

When I heard of this conversation I realised that the warmth shown by Mr Takeda after our talk together in the winter of 1942 was his sincere feeling and did not arise from any evil intention. Looking back I thank the Lord for the needed courage and faith that He gave me at that time. He truly fulfilled His promise in Matthew 10: 18-20, namely 'And ye shall be bought before governors and kings for my sake, for a testimony against them and the Gentiles. But when they shall deliver you up, take no thought how or what ye shall speak; for it shall be given you in that same hour what ye shall speak. For it is not ye that speak, but the Spirit of your Father which speaketh in you.'

Reflecting on that bitter struggle three years ago we gratefully and joyfully recall the grace of God who protected us and gave us such a glorious victory. But at the time the strain was intense. For who dare resist, even a little, the might of the Japanese military? I also recall a friend putting pressure on me at that time. 'Ming-dao' he said, 'I urge you even yet to learn a little wisdom. When the situation reaches a point where there is no alternative, a little more sacrifice will be worth it. But we have not yet reached the time for sacrifice.' I replied, 'If this is not the time for sacrifice then when is the time for sacrifice?'. But he continued: 'Are you not aware that for the Japanese military to kill a Chinese is no more than our killing an ant?' Listening to these words I momentarily felt fear clutch my heart. After a pause, however, I was able to answer him: 'What you say is correct, but I am not an ant. I am the servant of the most high God. Unless God permits, no one can harm me.'

As the year gradually wore away, my faith was sometimes strong and it was sometimes weak. Whenever I heard rumours of evil there arose in my heart a wave of fear. For my natural disposition is to be timid and weak. At the time of the Boxer rebellion my late father was overcome by fear and took his own life; I am his son. In this respect I am very much like my late father. The glorious victory which we experienced on this occasion was simply the great power of God being manifested in me. I have nothing to boast of; I boast only in the operation of God's faithfulness and of His power and might which is manifest in those who trust Him. My courage is small but the God whom I serve is incomparably great. There are those who say that I am fearless, but what they say is untrue. I have no natural courage whatsoever. Not fearless but fearful. The point is that what I fear most is giving offence to God. If I offend men they will undoubtedly rise up to harm me. But God has only to stretch out His hand and the rough places will become smooth, the danger will be turned into peace. On the other hand, if I give offence to God and He becomes angry with me so that judgement faces me, what will happen? Even if all the people in the world are minded to save me they are powerless to do so. It is not that I do not fear. It is rather that I fear God whom we ought to fear while I have not feared those whom we ought not to fear.

What I found most hard to bear in this spiritual conflict was not the violence of the evil forces but that the time was so prolonged. Had the period of battle been restricted to a day or several days, then it would have been infinitely easier. Even one or two months would have been bearable. But the time stretched from the first month of the year to the last. Every day for a long long time we were tossed to and fro on the surging waves. Our church was never closed, but we always had to be ready to meet closure; I was never arrested, but I always had to be ready to be arrested. Throughout the whole period we were attacked by Satan again and again. Only those who have experienced it can understand what that kind of suffering means. I am a human being. I have the thoughts of a human being, the feelings of a human being, the desires of a human being. I want to pass my time peacefully. I am afraid of physical pain and of adversity. I was acquainted with the cruelty of the Japanese Military Police; I knew that it was hard to endure the taste of imprisonment. My mother was nearly 80 years old and I was unwilling for her to be alarmed or frightened. But for the glory of God, for the church of God, and for the truth of God; for the doctrine to which I witness and for the Lord whom I serve, I cannot raise the white flag of surrender to Satan and go and do the things that the will of God and my conscience will not allow me to do.

I thank my God that His strength is made perfect in my weakness; that He ever leads me in triumph in Christ. I also thank God that my fellow-workers as well as my wife were of one mind with me. None of them hindered my actions; they were truly my joy and crown. Of the year 1942 I can say without fear of contradiction that well over 300 days were spent in the fiery furnace. Yet we were not alone. There was one with us like the Son of God. He who is the God of Shadrach, Meshach and Abednego, and the

God of Daniel, that God is our God too. Let us join to sound His praises!

(We have included this article as an appendix since it provides an excellent specimen of Mr Wong's ministry. It also is a fitting commentary on his own life as will readily be appreciated. It is from his "Spiritual Food Quarterly".)

11.
Smooth Stones...

by

Wong Ming-Dao

1 Samuel 17: 38-40, 48-51

All readers of the Old Testament are familiar with the story of David and Goliath. Goliath was the champion of the Philistines and he was feared by the whole army of Israel. Yet David killed him and so delivered the people of Israel from the Philistines. He did it with one small stone. Strange! Truly strange! The potentiality of one small stone was so vast that it could achieve deliverance for all the people of Israel. Obviously an important factor in this achievement was the skill of David in slinging stones. But most important of all was the fact that this was a marvellous act of God. For in effecting this deliverance God needed only one small stone to kill the champion — the fierce champion from whom everybody fled in fear. Similarly, when God effects deliverance today

He can use even the weakest of believers to achieve that which, without Him, is impossible even for an army.

The people around David were under the impression that only the use of the sword and spear and javelin could defeat a powerful enemy. But God made use of what man overlooked — a stone. Nowadays there is a common impression that it is only people with learning and ability and position and wealth who can achieve anything great. But God uses believers who are foolish and weak and poor and lowly to do wonderful things for Him. 'God hath chosen the foolish things of the world to confound the things which are mighty; and base things of the world, and things which are despised, hath God chosen, yea, and things which are not, to bring to nought things that are; that no flesh should glory in his presence' (1 Corinthians 1: 27-29). God could do wonderful things like this in days of old; He can do wonderful things today. He alone is worthy to be praised.

At the same time we are confronted here with a certain factor which we must not lightly dismiss. It is that when God used David to kill Goliath, the stones that David used were not ordinary stones; they were 'smooth stones' specially selected from the brook. Now the stones which lay in the brook were far too numerous to be counted; yet only a few of them were suitable for David's sling. Before David could go to the field of battle he had to make his way first to the brook and from the thousands of stones which lay there to select five smooth stones for his sling. He had to aim accurately and to hit the enemy's forehead. The stones had to be smooth. We must remember, however, that the process of making these stones smooth enough for use could not be compressed into a day. On the contrary it would require years and years of preparation.

The stones that we find in brooks or on the sea shore were originally thrown out as a result of huge explosions amongst the rocks. But all these stones at that time had sharp edges and corners. Not one of them was smooth. But as the flowing water swept over them they were constantly colliding with each other and constantly rubbing each other. In this way the corners were gradually rubbed off. As the process continued for thousands of years the stones in time became perfectly smooth. Now we often pick up stones like this both from streams and from the sea shore. But do we ever stop to think of the long process of friction which has made them so smooth? The more these stones were thrown together the more their corners were worn off and the smoother they became. At the same time they became more beautiful and more useful. Since stones are inanimate objects they have no feeling, and naturally we never associate the smoothing process with pain. But if stones had feeling when they were in collision with each other for such a long time I honestly do not know to what degree their suffering would extend.

The people whom God chooses and uses are in a similar situation. They have been saved, and the sins of the past have been forgiven, but many corners remain in their make-up. They are things like laxity, pride, selfishness, covetousness, envy, and hatred. Unless these corners are submitted to a long process of rubbing and buffeting they will not easily be removed.

The question arises, what does God make use of to carry out this process of rubbing? He uses the people around us. That which ceaselessly rubs and polishes a stone is not soil, sand, bricks, or pieces of wood; even less is it grass, leaves, cotton wadding, or sheep's wool. None of these things is hard like the stone. And none of them will ever rub off the corners. The stones are made smooth because they are constantly rubbed by other stones — vast numbers of them. Only hard things can wear out hard things. When the mountain torrents catch up the small stones and sweep them together they gradually lose their corners.

In the same way, for the corners in our personalities to be rubbed off we need to be thrown together with other people. I buffet you; you buffet me. By nature we like to live with people who are meek, peaceable, humble, patient, compassionate and benevolent. But God seems to go out of His way, as it were, to put us in the midst of people who are evil, violent, proud, irritable, self-centred and cruel. We murmur against God for not treating us more kindly; we lament that our lot is unpleasant; and we long to get release from our situation. We fail to perceive that God has purposely placed us in the midst of people like this so that the corners in our personalities, of which He is well aware, may in course of time be rubbed completely off. Without treatment like this the corners will remain. If you put a small stone with edges and corners into a ball of cotton wadding, even if it remains there for hundreds of years, the corners will not be worn down in the slightest. In the same way, if we live always among virtuous people our corners will remain with us — even perhaps until the Lord returns.

We often wonder why God persists in keeping us in unpleasant surroundings, in making us mix with unattractive people. For instance a man by nature wishes to take a wife who is virtuous and wise and submissive, yet contrary to his wishes the wife he marries is fierce and excitable. A woman by nature wishes to be married to a man who is gentle and considerate, but contrary to her desire she finds herself married to one who is churlish and rude. An elderly woman looks for a daughter-in-law who is filial and dutiful; but contrary to her hopes her son takes a wife who has no respect for her superiors. A young wife hopes to have a kindly mother-in-law, but contrary to her hopes she finds her husband's mother to be unreasonable and truculent. Masters desire servants who are loyal and obedient, but those they employ prove to be deceitful, cunning, and depraved. Servants wish to work for kind and considerate masters, but invariably they are cruel and repressive. Landlords fail to find good tenants; tenants fail to find good landlords. Superior government officials cannot find good subordinates; subordinate officials look in vain for good superiors.

So the general situation is most unsatisfactory. Reality rarely matches the ideal. God appears to be hostile to us and purposely loading us with trouble. But as soon as we understand the significance of the smooth stones our many suspicions completely vanish. Some of the people in our families are hard to get along with, and some of the people who share our courtyards are hard to live with, but God has expressly placed us among them so that they may help to rub off our edges and corners. In this situation all that we can do is to maintain thankful and obedient hearts and to endure the inevitable buffeting so that in the end we may become like smooth stones. We shall then be of great potential usefulness to the Lord.

Even though people treat us roughly, once we have understood the significance of the stones we shall cease to murmur against God. No more shall we opt prematurely out of our situation or seek to avoid the people who do not appeal to us. We accept God's perfect will and endure what He sends so that He can make us into smooth stones all the sooner. The pain which this prolonged buffeting brings to us may indeed be intense, but the advantages we gain by paying this price are such as can never be bought by silver or gold.

There are so many stones in the brook that you cannot count them. Yet in every ten you cannot find more than one or two that are useable. There was no room in David's pouch for the stones which had not been polished smooth. The process of attrition was essential. In the same way those believers who have not yet experienced trials and afflictions, and who have not yet been disciplined by God, are still not ready for His use.

We have seen, then, that David had to select five smooth stones from the brook before he went out to do battle. The question now before me is whether God, from this great gathering of believers, can choose five who are polished and smooth and prepared like the five stones of David. What I am even more anxious to know is whether I myself am qualified to be a 'smooth stone' in the hand of God.

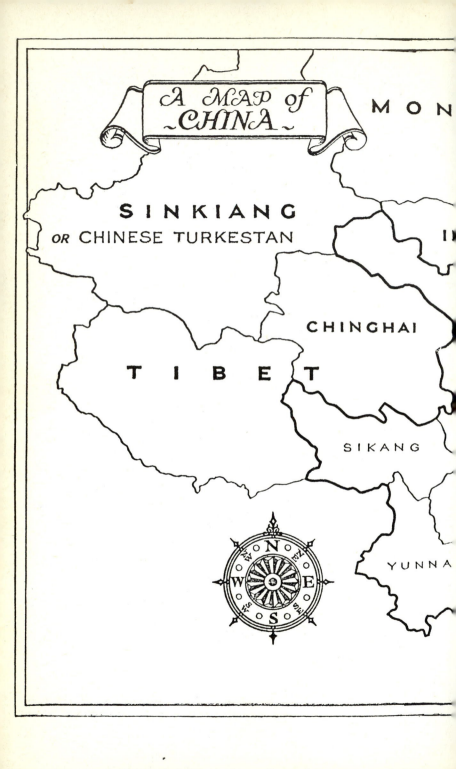

A MAP of CHINA

MON

SINKIANG

OR CHINESE TURKESTAN

CHINGHAI

TIBET

SIKANG

YUNNA

N
S
E
W

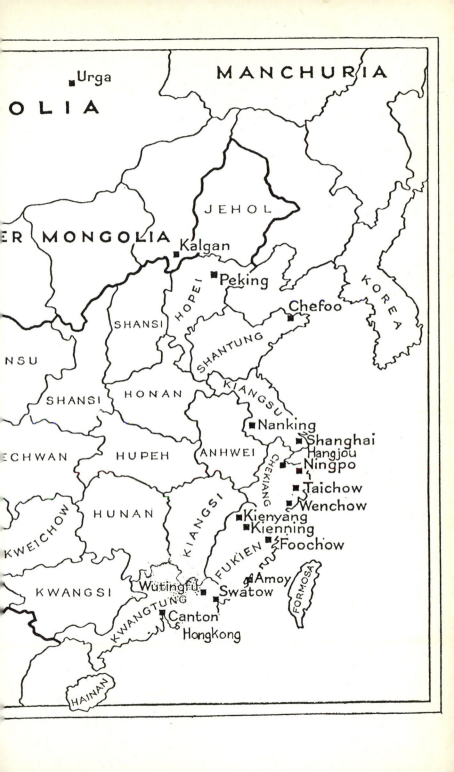